THE
DAYS
OF
TRAGEDY

FRANKLON RASHAUDE VOSS

authorHOUSE®

AuthorHouse™
1663 Liberty Drive
Bloomington, IN 47403
www.authorhouse.com
Phone: 1 (800) 839-8640

Published by AuthorHouse 08/24/2016

ISBN: 978-1-5246-2605-1 (sc)
ISBN: 978-1-5246-2604-4 (e)

Library of Congress Control Number: 2016913973

Print information available on the last page.

Any people depicted in stock imagery provided by Thinkstock are models, and such images are being used for illustrative purposes only. Certain stock imagery © Thinkstock.

This book is printed on acid-free paper.

Because of the dynamic nature of the Internet, any web addresses or links contained in this book may have changed since publication and may no longer be valid. The views expressed in this work are solely those of the author and do not necessarily reflect the views of the publisher, and the publisher hereby disclaims any responsibility for them.

TABLE OF CONTENTS

DEDICATION

Based on a true story about life in Dallas and Downtown Plano, Texas, this book is dedicated to anyone out there deep in the city streets. These are the days of tragedy, and in them, I'm delivering to you a message that cannot be refused. This message is for those who have experienced tough times and relied on the Lord to save them. Jesus Christ is our Lord and Savior, and He alone will save us from the terrible tragedies that are happening today.

This book is dedicated to the innocent people who are getting put down for no reason. It is a gift from Jesus Christ, and I am here to deliver this message. Trust in God and depend on no man. Pray for your soul and continue to live as the Lord says. Keep being a blessing and allow your light to shine in people lives. Keep being kind and generous to others. Keep praying for, caring for, and believing in the goodness of others. Continue to pray for the faithful ones who lead this country. Pray that they lead us out of the darkness and into the light. Pray that the Lord will continue to do his Wondrous Works in your life and in the lives of others.

This book is dedicated to my mother, Rachel Voss, who was an usher in church during my childhood and is now a church leader in the Women's Conference. If it were not for her, I would not be the witness of God and the Christian man that I am today. Thank you for being the Godly woman that you are and for leading me to Jesus Christ. During the times that Satan tried to attack me, success would have been his had you not instilled in me the belief in God. My strength came from you. To my family, thank you for believing in me. To my friends, thank you for supporting me.

Let this message be shared by everyone: Once you are in the Lord's hands, no one can remove you from His grasp!

ACKNOWLEDGEMENTS

Someone once told me that God is working on me and He is why I have written this message for you. Although I appreciate everyone who believed in my work and supported my vision, I offer a special thanks to Mrs. Tammy, the relative of my best friend, who believed in my book enough to offer her support in getting my message out there. I'd also like to thank my aunt, Flora Kynard, who helped me edit my book enough to take the next step. I owe my mother, Rachel Voss, another shout-out for the sacrifices she made to get the book accomplished.

To my best friends, Jared Brooks and Wyatt Gross, thank you for supporting me through this process. I would also like to thank my teacher, Mrs. Ford, for giving me her full support. She was the first person who really didn't know me, yet fully accepted me for who I was then and still am today. From the birthday cake you bought me when I was a young boy to your support with the writing of this book, your gifts have meant the world to me.

Thank you to everyone that gave me your full support in life and with the writing of this book. Were it not for people like you in my life, people who chose to love me though all of the trials of my life, none of this would be possible. Thank you to everyone who made the choice to be there for me though the good times and especially through the bad. Thank you all for the love and support through this entire process. I ask that God continues to bless each of your beautiful minds, hearts, bodies, and souls. Keep being the loving Christian people that you are.

Most of all I have to thank Jesus Christ for this gift. If it was not for my Lord and Savior, this book would not have come to be. When he first told me to write a book, my initial reaction was, "NO, I am not going to write a book." He told me again, and again, I said no! Then one day, without thinking about it, I picked up a journal and I began writing. This book was the result, and I owe all glory to God for the outcome.

INTRODUCTION

THE DAYS OF TRAGEDY

In my life, tragedies are occurring regularly. From day to day challenges to lies in my background records that try to keep me down, every day is a struggle. With God to guide me, I'm able to make it every day. I work hard daily from three o'clock in the evening to one o'clock in the morning. It takes two trains and a bus to get me there. My journey began as a young black man at a top notch high school, striving to graduate, and continued with me graduating from a small mechanic training academy. Thanks to the good Lord, my story is still being written today.

I would often hear my aunt and teacher tell stories of the tragedies that were happening around me. This fueled my drive to work hard every day of the week, so I could one day make it on my own. As I move forward, I will continue to work hard and remain strong, so that one day, I can stand on my own two feet.

I will continue to work hard, even here, in The Days of Tragedy.

CHAPTER 1

IN THE BEGINNING

I spent most of my days in high school talking with my friend and school teacher. I lived in North Dallas at the time. I had just moved to the area, and I remember that a drug king pin, one of many in that area, had been killed in a shoot out with the police.

Like any other high school, there were cliques. When I first arrived, some of the guys wouldn't let me hang out with them. That was fine, though. I had some friends of my own. We'd see each other at lunch time and go to the gym to play basketball. It was cool having my own crowd of friends. Although I was cool with all of them, only one of them was my true friend. We still hang out today.

Back in school, people use to wear these chains that the teachers would talk about. They referred to the chains as dog collars. I called them gangster chains. I knew I would get one as soon as I got a job. My first chain had the first letter of my name on it. I hated when people called them dog collars until I found out why. It was an army tag with a soldier's name engraved on it. When my friend, school teacher, and I would talk about what was going on the news, I would sometimes see them.

During our talks, I would sometimes tell my teacher terrible stories of things I'd seen. I recalled witnessing a sixteen year old fighting a policeman while trying to sell drugs. He was in the middle of the street battling police. When my teacher heard on the news what I said I had seen, she said that the boy was probably trying to get some attention. I think he was after more than that. Even though I tried to stay on the straight and narrow, I once got mixed up in some similar mess. When I got caught, I had to go before the judge. Thank God, the judge gave me a second chance. If he hadn't, I probably would have ended up in jail and dropped out of high school. When my teachers heard my story, they would often comment that I've come a long way.

I had one friend that was in a crip gang in high school. We had been close friends for years, so I influenced him to get away from the gang violence and into sports. I had finally convinced him! He got out of the crip gang and put his fighting spirit into high school football. At the time, I was a well-known basketball All-Star.

I had some other friends doing well in the army, but some of them were kicked out because they were fighting depression. One was yelling at other nice people, cursing out people at different places, and fighting. The army couldn't handle him anymore, so he was kicked out. We would talk about music, abusing women, and most of everything negative! My teacher said most of them don't know how to solve their own problems. I would sit back and listen to what she said, think about some things, and carry on.

People today say that the rate of African Americans who graduate and those who drop out is about fifty percent. When some consider how things are today, they would say that's not much. I hear it from so many people today. People on the news are talking about violence in schools. People in the streets are talking about what's wrong with our schools today. The big problem is that the people who are talking about the problems have the power to solve the problems, yet no one is discussing solutions. It doesn't make sense to talk about problems that are going on when you have the power to solve them. We need to improve the integrity of our young men and young women of today, and that begins with talking about where we go from here. If I had power, I would turn the tables around, but my resources are limited. I am just a young black man trying to make my own way in life.

For my 18th birthday celebration, one of my teachers bought me my first ever custom made birthday cake. Back then, my family couldn't afford things like that. During one of my parent/teacher/student conferences, my teacher started to cry as she was talking to my parents about me. She cried because she did not know what to do for me at the time. She asked me what I would like to do, and my response was simple: work. She said fine, and she found me some work to do. That's one of the times I will always remember. She was a nice older lady. I still visit her at the school every now and then.

When I graduated from high school, my family and teachers were there supporting me. My mother took pictures of me walking across the stage. People gifted me with congratulatory cards and money. My family came over to celebrate with me. At the time, I didn't think graduating was a big deal, so when I got my diploma, I asked my mom what I should do with it. She said, "You keep your diploma, and hang it on your wall." So, I kept it. I put it in my room, but I didn't hang it on the wall. I put it on the counter on a black stand.

As I made my way out of high school, my first job was at the grocery store. I started off bagging groceries. Women there kept telling me how nice I was. It was a rainy night, and everybody was tipping me. At the time I was working, and had gotten into college at the same time.

When I first entered college, my father told me if I want to do well, "You have to want to do well, and put your mind into what you are doing." I always remembered what he said and passed my first class in college. I had chosen acting as my major, but then I changed it. I decided I wanted to do something different.

Around that time, this gang of burglars had shot up a seven year old at a nearby school. My parents told me about it while I was working. I was thinking, "How can you do such a thing?" That child was not even old enough to ride a bicycle without training wheels. How could anyone kill children? Your mind has to be really messed up to kill an innocent child. People who do things like that are accusers of the devil, and are praising and worshipping Satan!

I use to see Satan. He was huge! He was an orange –like, reddish color. He had one of those back in the day, Jesus Christ, ancient history robes with a big sword, and big huge horns on his head. It scared the life out of me when I saw him. I was so scared, I think I used the restroom on myself. When I saw him, I was on the couch. I had just got up. I cursed out loud to myself. There Satan was staring at me. He was the ugliest thing I had ever seen. Ugly like an opossum! You know those big rats you can't stand to look at? He was ugly like that. He laughed and said, "I got you." He had a deep, demonic voice. He stood there, wanting to kill someone like he was God!

In that big, demon voice he had, he told me so many times to join Satan's army. I said no, and went to my room. Then he realized there was a Holy Bible in the room. He said out loud, "I hate the Holy Bible!" and left.

I know my sister heard Satan one particular night. She woke up the next morning saying she heard him. Then, she forgot all about it. It was Satan, the Prince of Darkness-a person that God does not love. Nobody wants to claim they've ever seen or heard him.

I started to understand as I got older because I found out what Satan was. I was thirteen years old when I first saw Satan. After I saw him, Jesus came to see me. It was twelve o'clock at night, and I was asleep. There was a big light in my room, so bright that I thought it was morning. Jesus had come to save me!

I looked behind me and saw a huge man standing there in a white robe. He had a beautiful, deep voice. At first, I did not know who he was. I asked him, "Are you a burglar who is going to kill me?" He said no! So, I asked, "Then, who are you?" He said, "Open your Bible to Genesis 1:1-2:7, and read it out loud." I read it and said, "You are God." He said, "Yes!" I was so happy! It was the happiest moment of my life! He told me so many things, but I had fallen into depression and lost my mind. I had forgotten everything he said, and I still wish I could remember.

As I was working, I was hearing less about negative things going on. I was starting to hear more about the positive. During my days working hard, people were telling me that we were going to have a black president for the first time. I was thinking to myself, "We are finally going to have a black President, despite all those days of slavery African-Americans had been through." I started thinking of all those great heroes like Martin Luther King, Jr., Malcolm X, and Rosa Parks. We have not had heroes like that in a long time. I was full of joy at the time I heard it. Dreams were coming true for many African-Americans. When Martin Luther King, Jr. and Malcolm X were killed, so many African-Americans went through problems because they did not know what to do. Back in the days of slavery, when African-Americans went through tragedies, they would get on their knees and pray and go to church every day. These days, some blacks often go to church and pray. Back then, the blacks made sure they went to church. I am probably assuming that blacks these days go to church less than the ones back in slavery, but I don't think I am assuming.

If someone was trying to beat and kill you, and that was acceptable by law, what would you do? I don't know. I would wish I was not living. The blacks in the days of slavery had God on their side, though, and they had success in everything they did.

The name of the man running for the first black president was Barack Obama. He had given the speech, "It's Time for a Change." There it was. The problems were about to end. Tragedy was getting ready to end because we would have a black president. In the middle of 2008, there it was, our first black president.

Dreams had come true for so many African-Americans. It was so amazing. The fact remained that we had been fighting against racism and slavery all these years. We kept getting all the broken pieces, yet we kept fixing them and putting them back together. You know African-Americans came a long way, from being beaten and killed for no reason, to here.

While Barack Obama was running for president, many people were talking about it. This guy I was working with was talking to me about it. The store manager had seen us talking. He had nothing to say. We both were black and he was white. A couple of days later, the guy had gotten fired for no reason. The manager did not catch me and other blacks talking, but he caught me and the one that got fired. That was the end of that guy. Now I was left doing everything at the store: cleaning restrooms, sweeping floors, and pushing carts.

After I graduated from high school, I was trying to get a good pay check. I was wondering how much a good check is, and a man told me. It was Valentine's Day, and I was mopping the floors real good. I had a scar on my face like Scarface had in the movie. I was real big, weighing 235 pounds, and I knew who I was.

I had come home at twelve o'clock at night. My mother had given me a paper saying "I Love You. Happy Valentine's Day." I was so mad and down from working hard, that I had taken my Valentine's Day thing down and stuck it under my bed, thinking nobody loves me.

During that time, things were not perfect for me. It was not perfect either for people having children getting kidnapped and killed in Dallas, Texas. It's taking someone you love away from you. Dallas was a dangerous place at the time. Too much was going on while I was trying to make it. I was hearing and seeing things that needed to be fixed. The best thing I could do was what my mom told me the day before Valentine's Day, "Keep your hands in the Lord's hands." When she told me that, I was like, "What are you talking about?" Another part of me was saying, "Yeah, I hear you." I was having my own moment at the time. Then I caught on to what it meant and I did it. I was holding on to the Lord's hands!

With us having a new president, I began thinking that we were going to have the young one's problem solved with the lounging pants. Most of the time it gets worse, but the change is finally getting ready to come. In Malcolm X's book, By Any Means Necessary, there were people on the streets that drank liquor, did drugs, and other things. They did not want to give into the Lord and go to church. I think it is the same with the young ones lounging their pants, but the young ones need to be educated. The people on the streets need God in their lives. Ha! I am a Christian that has been going to church all my life and God is awesome.

I was also thinking maybe the black president could fix the health plan, like helping us get the medication we take. If we could get a health plan that gives us medications, everything would be better at this time of our lives. It would be better for me if I was being well taken care of by my doctor I go to. When people look after you while you are in a slump, you feel a whole lot better, knowing things are taken care of.

Another thing that can be fixed is the banks. I didn't think my bank system was going well, but I was fine. Some people don't trust bank accounts. They will keep their money somewhere in a house. I felt the same way when I had got my first account. We are in the days of a tragedy that need to be fixed. Changes need to be made, and problems need to be solved. I don't have too much to say about banks, though.

You have many people not following the ways of life. In the Holy Bible, the Word of God says, "For the Commandment is a lamp. The Law is a light. The reproofs of instruction are the way of life." Those are the laws of life. Not everybody follows them.

We do the best we can but we have ups and downs. We have struggles such as trying to have less violence in this country and less hatred for one another, and trying to work with people who need help! Is that where we are today? Not long ago, some young man killed somebody over some money and some young guy harassed an elderly lady. I don't think these tragic times are only for African-Americans. We are all in the days of tragedy, and we have to do something about it.

To have little children getting murdered at the age of seven and eight is terrible. There's too much violence in the United States of America. I don't think anyone could fix it, especially with the way the days are going now. God have given us the Ten Commandments and one of those commandments is Thou Shall Not Kill.

We are not following his commandments in this country. We are following are own ways, not Jesus Christ's ways. Violence has been going on for years, and no one has put it to an end. If we don't fix what needs to be fixed, we are going down in a hard fall. We are already in a downward spiral right now in this world and country! Sometimes, we just don't know what to do.

People at the stores are starting to realize how good I am. They are offering for me to work in the meat market. A manager in the meat market starts to notice me while I am working up front at the store. One day I was mopping the floor and he saw me do it. He said, "I see how hard you work."

He asks me, "Do you go to school?" I said, "I am going to college right now." He said, "That's good, getting your education." Then he asked me a question. "Would you like to work in the meat market?" I said sure! He explained how he noticed how hard I worked and told me he needed a guy like me to stock meat.

He was going to put me in the meat market, and raise my pay wage to ten fifty an hour. That was what I needed in my hard days of work, a good pay wage. They had seen me there and realized how good of a worker I was. That was a blessing for me because some people did not want to pay me well for all the hard work I was doing. Everyone knew who I was because I worked hard every day of the week. I was everyone's friend. Everybody was crowding around me when they heard about it.

I was the first one talking about I want my money. When I started talking about it, everyone else started. Having people come up to me about the new job felt good. It was a good thing for me at the time. "It's time to get it together," I thought. It's a new start and things are going great for me. I felt like things were going the way I wanted them to go.

Hearing and seeing things around me, I knew great things were happening and time was about to change. Seeing everyone notice me working, they must have been saying, "He is a good man." Things were working out fine and I was strong the whole way.

People in the meat market were even coming up to me. It was great for me since I was just trying to make it at that time. Holding on to the Lord's hands makes a difference. I could see that things were getting better for me. I love the Lord with all my heart. He loves me before I love him. With that, I know I am going to make it in Dallas, Texas.

CHAPTER 2

CHANGES HAPPENING

"Did I get in or not?" I got in. I had got in and everyone was coming up to me, talking to me, and being with me. No one had any problems with me getting in the meat market. Changes were happening. We had our first black president at the time. Things were getting ready to change for the United States of America.

After I got the new job, the manager was showing me around the place so that I would know where everything was. Getting this job was a good thing for me because I had problems at the time. The government was putting lies on my background records. They were saying that I was not in school, I was mental, and I was not working! People saw how hard I worked and gave me a chance at something new. I had just got in the meat market, and I was making new friends already.

I had a friend around my age that I got along well with. I asked him about the new president. He said he would like him if he does what he said he would do. I told him he was going to do it, just hold on, but he was white and I was black. That was the difference between me and him.

While I was doing a hard day's work, the changes were happening. The new president was working on the health plan and banking system in the U.S. I was on medication at the time. That was not a bad thing for me. I had gone through some things, but I had made it out. Seeing the changes had been made, people started to talk and turn themselves around. I started smiling more, talking more, and having more conversations while I was working in the meat market.

I told the guy working about where I lived. He told me about a time when he knew a guy that worked at a store. The guy went outside to the curb waiting for somebody. He was standing there waiting, and some person was standing next to him. The person who was standing next to him pushed him off the curb and shot him in the head. Then, he got in a car and drove off. I didn't believe what he said. If it did happen, that is one of the most terrible things I have ever heard. If all this is happening, it is more than a tragedy, it is a crisis.

The way things are going on now, something needs to change around this country. The health plan would be good for everyone, not just the old people, I mean for everyone. I'm seeing myself in these kinds of days, just thinking, "What should I do?"

I spent time during the day praying that it would end one day and just hoping I would make it in Dallas, Texas. At the time, the President did not talk about the bank system, but he had handled the health plan. People were quitting and leaving, because it was all about the money.

See, the new days were coming forward, and everything was changing around me. Most of the people I knew were quitting because of the money. I did not ever think I would quit because of money. Everyone there liked me, but who knew what could happen.

While I was working, we were looking for a house we could live in. We had gotten tired of staying in an apartment in Dallas, Texas. We searched around Dallas for some houses. We did not find one at the time, so we kept looking. We found one next to us. It was a small, two story house. I liked it because it was still in Dallas. Most of the people knew who I was there. We did not think about buying the house. We would look somewhere else.

Around that time, I would go to an Italian restaurant called Fest Palace. They had some good food there. They had a five pound burger, chicken fried steak sandwich, two great big catfish dinners, and for dessert, Italian crème puffs. They knew who I was at the restaurant. They called me Bubba at Fest Palace. The Italian people there were like the people on the Godfather. They used profanity and everything else.

During these times, a man named Samuel talked to some guy that runs everything around the city. He had cursed out his wife on the phone, and the guy heard it. A few days later, the guy that runs everything around the city filed a report and closed Fest Palace down.

That was my hangout spot when I had days off college or work. I would go to Fest Palace to eat and hang out there or look at the news on TV. It could not get any better than Fest Palace! Even people in the office where I worked went there. I was still working in the meat market while we were looking for houses. We were having a great time in the market.

We would joke around while we were working. We would have fun conversations with customers while working. The managers would even be there. A few days later, we moved to where I came from in Plano, Texas. We moved back to Downtown Plano. That's the ghetto with a whole lot of black people.

They had people that would struggle down there and people that would go to church every day. In Dallas, where I lived did not have a church or a Boys and Girls Club. They had a great place for fun in Dallas, but no churches were I was.

My mother was a strong Christian woman who went to church. She and my aunt were the ones who got me to believe in Jesus Christ. That was my mother's older sister. My father was a guy who was into sports. He was a varsity player in high school and was in the newspaper and on television. Then he had opportunities, but he did not take them. I believe that's what stopped him from being a professional. Then, there's my sister. She is just a few years older than I am.

This time God is working everything out. One day soon, I will be the manager of everything that I am in. I take one day at a time, praying most of my days will get better. We had moved back to where I came from in Downtown Plano with my aunt. I had to take a train and a bus to work. It was no different there than Dallas.

I had seen things there just like in Dallas, Texas. One time, I saw a young black man get out of jail. I was sitting at a bus stop waiting for my bus to go to college. This young black man came up to us with a black eye with Vaseline on it, and lounging pants. He came to us talking about we are in the judgment day of Jesus Christ.

I was looking at him like, "What you talking about?" The girl next to us was white and she said we are not in judgment yet. He was explaining and saying we are in judgment. The conversation lasted about twenty-five minutes. Then the girl had told the guy to go off somewhere. Then he left with that beat up black eye and lounging pants.

You would not tell this to a Christian, but this girl did not know what the cross stands for. She had seen me with a cross on my neck and told me that does not mean anything. Seeing a cross with Jesus Christ hanging on it means that it is the crucifixion of Jesus Christ! Everyone knows what that means, yet on the other side, I am probably assuming. There are crazy things going on around some places. You can see it around those types of places if you just look around yourself.

As I was taking the train and bus, some black man said thank you to me. He was taking me to work on the bus. I had an army duffle bag that I took to work with my clothes and stuff in it. I took it with me everywhere, so I could change in and out of work clothes.

People would try to sell drugs like marijuana and others. They had this one guy that tried to offer me some marijuana. I told him that I did not want any. He walked off to other people and tried to sell some.

One day, I was standing next to the bus stop. It was a rainy day. There was a guy standing outside. His lips were moving real fast, and he was talking to himself like he was on cocaine. He probably was at the time.

I saw all these people lounging their pants and picking it up from other people. You would also have people try to offer you drugs. "Just say no when they come to you." There's no telling what that stuff would do to you. You would see all types of stuff once you got out there. My mother said to pray for them, but I was too busy trying to take care of myself.

While I was working in the market, some of the managers said I was getting complaints. They said I need to smile more and some other things about the job. To myself and others, I was doing a great job. For some reason there is something wrong.

It was getting ready to be New Year's and everyone was happy. I was working one night and a little kid was looking at the lobsters. I was talking to the kid and he would respond back about the lobsters. His mother saw me talking to him, and she would laugh at her son while he was talking and looking at the lobsters! I cannot remember the boy's name. He was a little white kid. Back then, I was a person you could look up to. All the little boys would come up to me. If I am still someone you can look up to, that is fine.

We had a hard day of work! I was thinking things are going to be fine at the time. Managers were talking about me. I would joke around with my friend at the market. I would tell him, "Say man, the hot mamas are looking for you!" I would tell him there is one outside saying, "Ooh, I Love You!" He would say I was lying. He would say, "You think I would go for that one, Franklon?" I would laugh and carry on. I would always mess around with the guys in the market. The manager in the market would mess around with me about the front store supervisor, but I am not going to talk about it here. I would get all types of complaints in the market, but everyone knew they were lies. Even though those lies came to me, we would still have our great times.

The New Year was beginning and everyone was getting ready to have a great time out. I came in to work in my Texas Rangers cap, all cool and stuff. That night, my friend said that he was going to the bar. Me, I just decided to hang around the house, chilling.

I would work out every day if I got the chance. I did what you call "pump iron." I could bench two hundred to two hundred fifty pounds. That would be my work out while I was in the meat market. I had shown my best friend what I was doing and he said it was awesome. I asked, "Do you want to work out with me." He said no, so I just had to move on.

A few days later, I got a good report from an undercover boss of the managers. I was a good worker. The manager pulled me in the office by myself and told me how good I was doing.

Me and the guys would talk about Jimi Hendrix, joke around, laugh, and have a good time. When I had some days off, I would pump iron in the back yard. I was starting to settle down and think about getting back in college. I planned on working in the market and going to college at the same time.

I was not just going to settle with what I was doing. I wanted to do more than I had done. I was reaching for the stars and I wanted more than I had ever imagined. Being a hard working man, people appreciated what I was doing. Everything was going the way I imagined. Seeing myself liked by everyone else made me real proud of myself!

One day, I was headed back to work. I got my bags and everything else ready to go. I was carrying my army duffle bag, and I saw a guy standing at the curb. I knew who he was. I asked him, "What are you doing here?" He said, "I am still running the hood," with profanity. I thought to myself, "Lord Jesus, he is still in this neighborhood acting crazy." He was skinny and weak as you know what. The only thing he looked like he could run was a flap jack pancake. I was walking to the train station and I started to get a little dizzy and woozy. I got on the train, and started to swiftly drift away. I was sitting back like someone had shot me in the chest, like in a gangster action movie. If my eyes could have gone to the back of my head, they would have. I had been shifting and drifting away during the whole train and bus ride. It was like I was hearing the sweet old, classic music, flying, dying, and going to heaven. I made it to work with my army duffle bag, my original clothes and everything still in it!

I was working hard, but I was having a bad time. The managers pulled me in the office to talk to me about some things. I wondered what it was about. It was nothing but lies to just put me down. They made up a lie, talking about I had too many complaints. At the time, I had good reports from undercover bosses, saying that I was a great worker.

They put me in the office with everyone around me like I was in a gangster movie! I was black and everyone else was white. It was a racism thing. I was going to tell the manager I quit right there in his face. Instead, he boosted himself up like he was going to hit me in the face. He tried to make me say I was putting in my two weeks' notice! Bull! I quit working at the store and went looking for other jobs. I did not have a job. I went back to work with my father as a janitor. I had gone to two different cities mopping floors and other things.

I would get sixty dollars in my pocket every week. I would just go out and buy CDs and movies. I would buy some body building vitamins so I would get bigger. It worked out fine; you just have to be careful about what you take.

I would sit back and relax, hearing the sweet old music! I would always find some music to listen to and just spend my days hearing the sweet old music. I felt like I was flying in the sky and no one would catch me.

Sometimes, I walked up and down the streets singing old music! I enjoyed my days playing music in the car while me and my neighbor talked all day and all night. I had gone to a CD store in Dallas, where I use to live. I bought a James Brown CD, and I got a free CD with it. The free CD I got was Marvin Gaye's "What's Going On" Special Edition CD. I also got that CD my neighbor told me about, Marvin Gaye's "The Marvelous One."

We would sit outside until ten o'clock, playing that CD every day and every night. That is one of my best memories. I enjoyed just hanging outside with my neighbor. I was doing well at the time.

Around this time, the president was handling the banking system. He was putting billions of dollars in the banks, just trying to get things right. During the time, I was hanging out at a bar up the street. It was one of the most crowded places I had ever been to! They had music outside; they had bars, and other things.

I would just hang outside and talk to the women there. I was not old enough to get in, so I just hung outside and talked all night. I was just twenty years old. I'd go to the bar and talk to these women all night long, just chilling and hanging outside.

I met a couple of women and I talked to them all night. I was just having fun! I would talk all night at the bar, until I met this particular girl. I started to call her my girlfriend! We would meet at the bar every night.

We talked about the games that came on television and other things that were going on. One night, we were outside of the bar talking. Then, we saw this fat guy who was on cocaine. He was about to fight a girl.

He was disrespecting her and she did not like it. They were about to fight but they didn't. She walked off, but he was still talking trash. Then, the fat man finally backed down. He saw a guy in a car and started yelling. Then, he went to the bar front door with some girls he knew. The fat man went up to them and sniffed some cocaine up his nose. He had his pants and boxers pulled down with his butt showing. He finally jumped in a car while it was driving off, with his butt hanging outside the window.

I just stood there on the side with my friend, watching all of this. It was like an action movie, with all this stuff happening. Meanwhile, my twenty-first birthday was coming up. I was enjoying myself all of this time.

I told my friend that I was turning twenty one soon. She said, "When you turn twenty-one, meet me inside and have your favorite beer." My favorite beer was Budweiser. I told her alright, then quit showing up for a few days. I was just sitting back, hearing the sweet old music.

During the day, I walked around outside thinking of all the things that were happening at that time. I looked at the news and all types of things were happening. A lot of little children were getting murdered in those days. There was too much violence in this country.

I was still thinking to myself, "How can you do a thing like that? You must have a terrible mind to kill an innocent child. You are really sold out to the devil if you are doing something like that. More likely than not, you are working with Satan!

They have a saying in church: Nothing but the righteous shall see him. I believe in that saying. Just a few days later, I would have my twenty-first birthday. My mother kept reminding me about it. Again, I just sat back, hearing the sweet old music.

I was no longer working at the store. Everything had changed around there. Some of the stores had closed down. They made a pizza shop next to the restaurant I use to go to. There also used to be a shop that would teach you how to play poker and other casino games that you could play in Las Vegas.

The whole area where I worked had changed. People that used to work with me didn't work there anymore. They had gone to other places to try to make better money. Most of the front end workers now worked somewhere else. Changes were happening at that time. I did not even realize that the changes were happening.

Then, it was my birthday! I was finally twenty-one years old. My family was happy to celebrate with me. My mother bought me a birthday cake with my name on it. It said "Happy Birthday, Franklon!" We had some candles on top for me to blow out. As I blew out the candles, I struggled with one. Finally, I blew it out.

I said that last candle was like Tina Turner, still lasting. I said that because Tina Turner was seventy-one still making that good music. I wanted the new CD she had put out. I wanted it, but I didn't think I would find it. Everyone was having a good time, and it was my twenty-first birthday. I had been moving around, just doing things to keep myself out of trouble. My birthday had passed and I was looking forward to great days happening.

I was singing a song, moving on with joy in my days. I stopped going to the bar for a while, and I stopped seeing my friend. Around that time, I would write down every day that I went to the bar. Then, my laptop broke and I forgot what days I would go up there.

Working with my father kept money in my pocket. I would also go to the mid week church service. When I first went, I told them it was my first time at mid week service. I told them that I would go to the park and spend time with the Lord, reading the Holy Bible.

Sometimes I missed mid week service to try to put some money in my pocket. I would hear the sweet music, and then look at the moonlight and stars every day I went to the bar. I really missed my friend. I wished I could see her again. I was pumping iron to keep strong. I kept hearing that song "Sweet Music, Sweet Music, you are the Queen of My Soul." Wearing a t-shirt and drinking a beer, I remembered the days that I would get out and hang at the club. I was not even old enough to get in then. I saw so much out there. I once saw a woman that looked like the first black president's wife. I said to myself, "That woman looks like Michelle Obama." Then I said to myself, "There's no way in the world that would be her in Downtown Plano!" I was having a good time.

I sat around, wishing everything was going right in the meat market. If everything was going the way it was supposed to be, everyone would be happy. We could joke around and have good conversations with the customers and other workers, and everything else would be good.

Then, those days went away and everyone else went off on their own. Changes were happening at that time. I was on the move, trying to make it.

CHAPTER 3

HOME SWEET HOME - BACK WHERE I CAME FROM

Home, sweet home, back where I came from! I was working with my father, and I still made it to mid week service. Working with my father kept me out of trouble. I went to work with him and stayed positive, thinking good things about myself.

I walked around talking to friends that would not put me down. I was back home, sweet home-back where I came from. Back in the ghetto! I called it Downtown Plano. That was where I had my very first best friend. My best friend's mother and my mother grew up with each other.

I would go down there sometimes to play basketball, back in Downtown Plano. I only went to the bars in the daytime. I would just throw some darts at the dart board and hang out. I started hearing all types of things on the news.

I heard about nothing but killings by people. It was so bad that a man shot up some children in a van. The killing situation was getting worse and worse. We were walking in the days where there were a lot of killings going on. Violence was one of the main tragedies.

Sometimes I felt I wanted to cry. My mind was thinking of enemies who were trying to put me down, making me want to cry and give up. I didn't stop. I just kept going. What I would do is get me a twenty-four ounce of Budweiser, start drinking the whole bottle, and try to stay strong the whole day. Staying strong everyday was hard! I would walk down the street with a Budweiser without a bag, and show it off while the police were looking at me! That's how bad it was.

I could not keep up with working and mid week service, so I started going to Bible study. I went to Bible study for the first time and it was good. It was on Tuesday of every week. That was a good thing for me. I was going every day of the week, and working with my father. Things were going great for me. I could see myself really trusting in God. That put a smile on my face!

I was going back and forth trying to find some more work. I went to the shelter to see if they needed help. They said they would like some help. Then, I went back and forth trying to see when I could work. I really didn't start working at the shelter, but I thought I would be fine.

When I was going to Bible study, we talked about the Flesh of Law of Sin. We would talk about it every week. Then we would talk about what we should do. The Bible study teacher looked at me. What are we supposed to do? I said, "We are supposed to do the ministry for the Lord." That was what I actually said. She said that was correct. We are supposed to minister for the Lord.

I was starting to get my own thing together and handle my own business. We started talking about being in vain. We talked about how you are in the flesh if you are blaming everything on and cursing to God. I had never thought about blaming, cursing out, or anything else, to God.

I was going to the library every day, and hitting baseballs in the park. I was just going back and forth to the park. I would see a man in front of the library. He would just curse at and blame everything on God. He was in vain in the flesh. I went to Bible study where we would have a meeting and talk about it, but I was actually seeing it. I did not talk about it. I would see this man at the library, and he was in vain in the Flesh of Law of Sin! I went back the next week, just looking at everyone else.

When I went to prayer request, I told everyone there was a man in vain in the Flesh of Law of Sin, blaming and cursing at God! They said, "Let us pray." We prayed for an hour. Then, we all went home. The next week, I went to library and the man was gone. All of that cursing and blaming everything on God was not worthy of anything.

He is Almighty God, Jehovah, God of Gods, King of Kings and Lord of Lords, Sovereign Lord, The King of Glory, and The Lord and Savior. How can you blame anything on God? I could not even imagine something like that. God is just too good to me.

I can't help but to say I love you, Sweet Jesus. It says in the Holy Bible, "Hear ye, He speaks of excellent things and the opening of his lips come out the right things." I jumped when I read that in the Bible. It gave me guidance. It feels good to know how good the Lord is.

I just went on moving forward. I didn't talk about that man. There's no telling what the man was doing now. I was just there, hearing and seeing things, in the days of tragedy. I sat down and talked with my aunt, because I was thinking about getting off my medication.

My aunt was telling me to stay on my medication, but I still thought about getting off. I thought I was doing well, but I was doing badly at the time. My body had gone into shock, and I thought someone was trying to hurt me.

I would think all types of things. I would think someone was trying to get me and that somebody is talking about me. I would think all type of things. I always had been thinking someone was trying to put me down. At the time, I was thinking it and no one was doing it.

Satan and the enemy were trying to take over my mind. They did not do it because God did not allow it to happen. I had got back on my medication a month later. Things were going pretty well and I was in church every day.

I would pray every morning before I went to church. I was seeing a lot of things that people would talk about. I was a serious type of person with a lot of faith and courage. I would build my self-esteem up. I usually don't have any problems when I run into different people.

When you walked outside at some places, you had to walk like you mean something. If you don't walk like you mean something, guys are going to beat you up. You can't walk around the areas where I stay at like you don't mean anything. Those guys would beat you down.

Sitting at home looking at the news, there was nothing but violence. You would see nothing but killings of innocent children. I would go outside, get the newspaper, read, and there it was in the news!

People were killing innocent children. There was so much chaos happening with this tragedy! I would go to Bible study and think about it. I would just want to do a prayer request for the children around the world. I would get on my knees, and pray for the world the way it was.

I would just pray sometimes for the world. It says in the Holy Bible, "When the Lord comes, he will restore the earth the way He had it." I just smiled when I heard the Word of God. It was good to hear the Word of God. It also says in the Holy Bible, "And the Lord said, "Thus speak said the Lord. Thus speak of the Lord. Speak of Israel, everyone come to you. Everyone in your mind!" I take that Word of God and replace it with something I talk about.

Then, I would just talk about God all day. That's what kept me doing well! A few weeks later, I would keep going to Bible study not saying anything. Another few weeks later, I would be sitting next to someone. That's usually what went on at Bible study.

When we get to the prayer request, I would still not say anything about it. I would just be silent and sit back not saying anything. Then, someone in Bible study would just make a prayer request. There was this woman that I would sit by. She would have a prayer request for this nation.

She would say in her prayer request, "I would just like to have a prayer request of this nation and what is going on in this nation." I would just stand there and listen to what she had to say. I was thinking about the children getting murdered on the news. At the time, I was just not saying anything about the young children. I would go to Bible study, and just be as silent as I could be.

When I would go home, I would sit down and play the video game all night. I would just sit in the backyard with the fireplace going and the moonlight shining with the stars all bright. I just sat back relaxing and enjoying myself in the backyard! I was thinking to myself, "What a beautiful night out, with the moonlight all bright and the stars shining as bright as they can be!" I wondered what it would be like if everything was going right.

Things would have changed by then. Everyone would be happy if everything was going right. At the time, though, everything was not going right, so what we needed to do was just pray for what's happening.

I know I am not crazy. People call me crazy, but they are liars. I knew everything would be going great and it would be fine. Actually, it was going right. I think you have to be like that woman I sat next to at Bible study, and just go ahead and pray for this whole nation.

When the Lord comes, He will restore the earth the way He had it. When Jesus Christ comes! When the Lord comes back again! When the Lord comes! That is what I am talking about. Not too many people will accept Jesus Christ as Lord and Savior.

It is sad if you cannot just accept Jesus Christ as Lord and Savior. Making my way back to Bible study, we would still have meetings about the Flesh. Then, I was still silent about praying of the killing of innocent children, but that woman was not struggling to pray for this nation.

This nation had too much violence, hatred, jealousy, and was accusing each other for our problems. I say only the Lord can save this country. The way everything was going, everyone needs God. Every week I went to Bible study, she was praying for this nation.

I finally said something, but it was not for the innocent children getting killed. I prayed for the enemies, that they would be in the Lord's hands. That was the only thing that I prayed for. I started to move on in my days.

I sat, just thinking about some of the things going on. I tried just keeping my head straight every day, thinking something good was going to happen. I was a young man trying to make it out here in this world of violence.

Trying to make it is hard these days. There are not any jobs that will have you working for some good money. It is hard to get a job these days. Not too many people have jobs. If you have a job, you better keep that job and hold on to it. Then, wait till things get better.

These days, you have to get an education if you want to get somewhere in life. It is hard just trying to get out on your own. While I am moving on in these days, I will just keep my head straight and just keep going.

Saying the Lord's Prayer cleared up my path way. His word is a lamp for my feet and a light for my path. The commandment is a lamp. The law is a light. There are the reproofs of instructions for the ways of life. I could see myself in these days!

We are in the days where things that are wrong are the things that are right. Wrong is right! Right is wrong! Wrong is right. In these days, we are not following the Lord's commandments and laws. The Lord has spoken to the people about doing what he said. That's the way some people are. We are in the day where right is wrong.

Back when I was little, I would get a whipping for just taking a cookie. Man, I mean I wanted a cookie. They would just whip me for that. I would get whippings for no reason. Today, they let little children do anything they want to do.

The children talk back, beat up their parents, and even kill their own parents. These days are nothing but foolishness. People are always blaming people for other things! They are probably not even a part of the reasons in this country where wrong is right.

There is nothing but foolishness in this country. God doesn't have time for foolishness. Most of all, the foolishness comes from Satan. God put the devil out of heaven for a reason. The Lord doesn't have time for Satan's foolishness.

The Lord Jesus Christ doesn't have time for foolishness; that is what I say. I was getting up one morning, and just thinking about the times that I have been out, and what I have seen. I saw someone getting out of jail, people lounging their pants, drug addicts, and even homeless people.

I started to think about doing something. At the time, the only thing I could do was pray. Seeing people on cocaine and other things, the only thing I could do was pray. I had started to pray my life away. Praying, praying, and praying every day. During the day I was praying. I was just going on a rampage. I was just praying real loud, heavy, and steady.

I would get up and nobody would bother me. One day, I was just praying, praying, and praying out loud. Then, when I finished, I went to the park and felt the Holy Spirit. The Holy Spirit was looking over me.

I felt the Holy Spirit. That feeling felt good at the time. It felt good all the time. I felt the Holy Spirit and I wanted it to stay with me forever. Having the feeling of the Holy Spirit was the greatest feeling.

I could remember at the time we had a church saying, "There's nothing like the Holy Ghost because the Holy Ghost party doesn't stop." That is how good it was.

Still working with my father, I was getting paid sixty dollars every week. I was doing good working with my father. I was just keeping myself out of trouble. There were problems where people couldn't keep themselves out of trouble. I would be the one that kept me out of trouble. Nobody would bother me! I always had my head straight, so I could keep myself out of trouble.

I was always praying that things would get better in this country. I just kept walking in the Spirit of the Lord, as the Holy Bible says, just keeping my faith, hope, and love alive! I would hear all types of things going on, but there was no one trying to stop it.

Having the faithful ones to do his work is good. At the same time, everyone is waiting for the Lord to come. In these days of tragedy and this spiritual warfare, we have to pray our way out. Sometimes we go through things that make it hard to live our lives. So much is going on. So many things are happening, yet people just don't know what to do.

Some people are lost in this world, and they don't know which way to go. When people are lost, they will sometimes go the wrong way in life. It is best when you are lost to put your hands into the Lord's hands. That is the best thing to do all the time: keep your hands in the Lord's hands. Yes Lord! Keep your hands in the Lord's hands. I use to see myself everyday having my hands in the Lord's hands. That's the way to go.

I got up one day and went walking down the street, just singing the Christian song "Amazing Grace!" I turned my head and looked, and someone had got in a car wreck. It was like Jesus Christ was telling me something. All I know is that I was walking down the street singing the song, and when I looked up, a car wreck had just happened.

Maybe I had to pray about it. Only the Lord knows! He knows what you think, what you are going to do, what you are going to say, and what is going to happen. Only the Lord knows! That is the whole truth, only the truth, and nothing but the truth.

I read the Holy Bible as much as I can. I plead the Flesh and Blood of Jesus Christ all over me. If we would be living in the Truth, it would be different. Right now, we are living in the darkness just a little bit!

We are trying to make it to where we are living in the truth, but we are having some struggles. We have to pray about everything we do and everything that is happening. I'm still walking in the spirit of the Lord and keeping my head straight, hoping that something good would happen in my day! So much is going on in this country. There is hardly anyone to do anything about it. Are people really trying to do what they need to do?

I was visiting Dallas where I was playing Jimi Hendrix. A woman said that they gave Elvis Presley and Jimi Hendrix all these medications. If they hadn't, then there would be nothing wrong with them. Some of those medications people give to you are not good. She said some people would pretend to do something for you, but they would get your money and turn you down the next day.

Having someone to do something for you can be scary! I would not trust in them at all. I would put all my trust in God. At first, I did not trust anyone. I did not trust my father, mother, sister, or anyone. I had trust in God and myself.

I felt like I could not trust anyone, so I put my trust in myself. It is not about the way you feel, but no one would have said that. We are in the days of tragedy, hoping that we would be living in the truth.

Praying that we would be living in the truth goes a long way. That's the way God wants us to live, and we have to do everything according to the Word of God if we want to live in nothing but the truth in this life. Sometimes life is war and every day is a battle we have to fight. We have battles in our mind and at other places and stages. We have battles with some people, but they would be our enemies.

Around this time, I would go out looking for jobs. I was looking for mechanic jobs. I would search here and there. I went to every mechanic shop that was near my house. I would fill out where I went to high school, but it was not the right place. They were looking for mechanic schools, so they would not give me a job.

Employers called my house at the time. I would not know what to do, so my Aunt started to look for a school. She found a mechanic training academy. Then, I found a school to go to, so I would get the job. I went to school, and it was a new way for me to progress. I got myself ready for this new phase. I was on the move.

CHAPTER 4

A NEW PHASE

When I first went to the mechanic school, I tried to get everything set up. The school was a small mechanic school. It was near a junkyard in Downtown Dallas. It was a long ride from where I was from. My mother, sister, and I had gone to Downtown Dallas.

I did not know where it really was. I did not think well about it all. I was thinking it was like one of those places big time gangsters would go to. Big time gangsters probably would go to a place like that.

Then again, the only time they would go to a place like that is when they would probably kill someone. They would take someone to the junkyard, and just torture, kill, and then destroy a man

It was that type of place to me. I might be assuming thinking it is just me. My mother, sister, and I had gone there. I did not think it was a school at first. I just thought it was a junkyard, but it was not. We went inside the building. There were people sitting down and standing all over. I walked in and there was a woman that was an assistant. She said, "How can we help you?"

My mother and sister said, "We are trying to get him in school. Is this the mechanic training academy?" She said yes. Then she got one of the owners. We all talked. We had a conversation about me getting in the school.

The man we met was the full time owner. He was also the teacher. We talked for about an hour about how to get me in the school. He said, "Get a counselor to help you get in the school. The counselor will help you pay to get in school."

It was like financial aid when you have the counselors help you. That is the only thing he told us. Then, we had to figure out how I was going to get there. They had a map showing all the places around the city of Dallas. He showed us how to get there on the map. I was looking at the map. They told us to get on the train and bus to get there. I got my train and bus tickets from my counselor. Then, we talked and left the school.

I was sitting home thinking, "What I did get into?" I really thought about not going to the school. Then again, I thought about trying to make it. A few days later, we went to see my counselor. We went to the counselor building. We had a meeting there to sign papers.

I signed some papers and they gave me a counselor. I had a meeting just for a day. After that, we had to see our counselor. I had seen my counselor just a few days ago when we had a meeting about getting in school.

She was a nice woman. She asked me questions about the school. Where does it take place? I told her that the school was in Downtown Dallas. It is a small school. She said she would need more information about it, so I had to go get some information and give it to her. We left the counseling office and went home. I did not think well about going to this school. I probably thought I could do something else, but I went anyway.

I was sitting down looking at the news and things were going fine. The day looked pretty good. There was nothing bad going on at the time. It was nice day, the sun was shining, birds were singing, and everything was going nice.

I settled down at night time. I went in the backyard. Then, I lit up the fireplace and just sat back and relaxed all night. Around that time, we were getting ready to move in a new house. The new house was next door to us. I did not say anything about it. I thought we were going to move farther off. We were just going to move in the house next door.

A month later, we moved into the house. It was a beautiful house. Before we moved into the new house, they had to remodel it. It took a month and a few days to do it.

I would just go to the gym and play basketball every day. I was good at basketball. I was a middle school All-Star. I played in the 7th, 8th, and 9th grade. I did not get to play in the 9th grade because of my grades, but I was still on the basketball team.

I use to have scouts looking at me, but those days are gone. Now, I am in the days were everyone is struggling. The days are going wrong now with so much violence going on! When I was younger, there would be hardly anything going wrong. These days, everything is going wrong. People today pray that the Lord will come.

When it comes time for everyone to see the Lord Jesus Christ, I believe everyone will try to get saved. My mother said, "I don't think everyone will get saved." I had a different thought from my mother. I had the joy of seeing the Lord and just being there with Him the whole time.

In our life, He is with us all the time. He says He will never leave us or forsake us. That is the word we need to hear every day. I shall not have the spirit of fear, so therefore I walk with the Lord with his rod. I read that verse in the Holy Bible, but I can't remember the chapter it is in.

I was getting ready to make progress at a new phase! In a few weeks, we had another meeting with the counselor. We talked and it was about getting financial aid. We had a thing called FASFA. It was a financial service to help you get in school. I filled it out from the beginning and it looked fine. Then, I started to fill the rest of it out. It would not let me fill it out.

I went back to the counselor. She knew what to do. She asked other people that had gone to the same school I had. Then, she kept finding out more about it. They paid for the entire school program.

They paid for the entire school program that was ten thousand dollars to get in. They had paid for the train tickets and all. The whole thing was free to do. It was a small school, so I would understand.

I had got into ITT Tech, but it cost forty five thousand dollars to go. It was too much at the time, because we were trying to get the house. I wanted to go to ITT Tech as a business man, but it was too much money. It was forty five thousand for an Associate Degree.

I wanted to be an architect. It was one of those things I was used to seeing. My father was a janitor for an architect company. They had movie theaters, restaurants, and arcade places. It was a great thing to do. There was good money in it. Sometimes you would get more than ten thousand a pay check.

I was going to this school as an opportunity, because everything was free. A few weeks later, I was going to school. I was in Downtown Dallas, at a mechanic training academy! The school was small and near the junkyard in Dallas. We would work on automobiles at the school.

When I first went there, I got lost near the railroads. I started walking. Then, I got to a point where I thought I was at the shop. I got on the railroad tracks, and I started walking and running on the railroad tracks. I had a phone in my pocket, but I lost the phone. Then, I got to a real far off point at the railroad tracks. I ran into a man. He said, "What you are doing?" I said I was looking for a school.

He said, "It is not here. Get off my railroad." I got off and went on the bus and took the train home. I called back when I got home and told them I had gotten lost. I tried to go back the next week. The next week, I went back to the school.

There was an easy way of getting there. Then again, I had gone the same way. This time, I had not gone on the railroad. I talked on the phone to the people that work there. I was talking to them and finding my way to the school. I walked all the way to the end of the railroad tracks.

I got back on the phone and talked again. They said, "See the second tower? Walk to the second tower and there is the shop." I did not see it, so they sent the owner to get me. I called back and started to walk all the way down till I saw the tower. I walked to the shop and saw the owner.

I went on and walked in because I was already there. I went to the school for my first day. I wore a Polo sweater and some jeans to school. I saw a bunch of people sitting down talking. The owner said we have Life Skills in the morning. Every morning, we would have Life Skills. We had Life Skills, and then we went to work.

They had an instructor there. He was a nice man. All the people were nice there. They would have prayer every morning that we had Life Skills. It was like a Christian school. Were they just having nothing but God in it?

They did not allow rap music, rock n' roll or anything else! The only music they had was the symphony. They were just trying to keep things going right. I had gone for my first day. It was all right! Then, on the other days, I would witness things that other people would talk about every day.

29

It was things that people were just having problems seeing. Some of the people would try to fix it. Some people would leave it saying that is just the way it is. While I was going to school, I would try to do something so that the people would know we would do the best we can. When we were in church, I was praying in tongues, but when I got to school, I was silent.

CHAPTER 5

MAKING PROGRESS

As I got in the Training Academy, the government quit sending us letters talking about I was mentally challenged, not in school, and not working. At night, I got ready for the morning time. I got up at 5 o'clock in the morning to go to school. It was a long journey to the school. I was just praying in tongues when I first went there.

It was a crowd of people still sitting down and we would get into Life Skills. Then after Life Skills, we would pray. We would have the Word of God, and then pray after the word. It was a beautiful thing that you could go to a school and have prayer in a school!

My aunt used to tell me that they had prayer in school. It was in a chapel. Every morning, they would round up the kids and have prayer in the school like we have the pledge. After we had prayer, we went to work. We started taking apart cars.

We started working and pulling out engines. I had to just examine and observe when I first got there. I had to wait till I got my tool box and clothes from school. The school gives boots, clothes, and a tool box so you can work on the cars.

I was getting help to go to school for free. I was an individual by myself who had hardly any friends and hardly any people to hang out with. Going to this training academy was an opportunity.

My aunt said there were opportunities out there for us young people. Back then, they did not have many opportunities for blacks. Back then, they were putting us down-beating us, killing us, and hurting us for no reason. Today, we young African-Americans have opportunities.

Just going up there for the first time was a journey. I had to keep my head up and straight just to walk in Downtown Dallas. It was tough going into the Downtown area. I went to Bible study at church on Tuesday. I was witness to all types of things happening on the train and bus to school! I saw young people that did not really care for themselves, acting crazy, fighting, and getting in trouble.

I was in Downtown Dallas, the deep areas. I had come to Bible study with something on my mind. I wanted to let people know what was going on. We were in Bible study talking about condemnation. It was a good conversation that people were in to.

I was in my seat with everyone at the table. It was a good Bible study. We all enjoyed it. I went home, and got ready for tomorrow.

I got up in the morning, praying! It was a journey to go on the train. I had made it to school. We waited for a while to have Life Skills. When we had Life Skills, the teacher was talking about how bad of a condition this country is in. He talked about it for an hour.

I was in shock when he talked about it. I was wondering why he was saying that. He was only telling the truth. This country was about to go into a down fall. We are trying to do everything by ourselves. As a country, we are not working together.

We were trying to do things ourselves and not trying to help one another. I was thinking, "Why is he talking like this?" but it is the truth I am hearing. We were the greatest country out of all countries, but from what I am hearing we are in a down fall.

I was stunned from what he was saying. I did not think out of all these great things we have going on in America-The United States of America-that we would ever have that problem. We got through with Life Skills, but I was stunned the whole time. When he talked about the country, I had my mouth shut from what he had said.

I went on the bus and it was crowded. It had a lot of blacks on it. Of course, it is Downtown Dallas. There were people struggling for money and violence all around.

I was witnessing the young people at that time. I had started to get some thoughts together about the problems of young men and women. I had to get everything set up and ready for the next day.

I had awakened that morning. I said a prayer before I left. I got on the train and my day had begun. I was headed to Downtown Dallas with all these life problems people talk about every day. I had made it to the school. We would all gather in the morning and get ourselves ready for Life Skills. The teacher talked about the country again. I was still stunned from what he said the other day.

That was not the end of the talk. He had begun talking about the economy or something. He said that if we start to help one another, we would all be doing well today. If the countries would just quit putting each other down, we would not be in the down fall we are in today.

If we don't quit looking at one another, just standing there when we really need help, it would be a better place than what it is today. We are just waiting for each other to fall, and we just stand there not helping each other.

I was getting riled up, from what he had been saying. I thought I would not hear anything bad about this country, but I heard it. The only other thing I heard is that it is time for America to change. I heard that speech from Barack Obama.

It was time for a change, but I did not know all of this. He was saying if we don't stop putting down one another, we are going to continue to fall as a country. He said we are in a down fall.

I kept praying every morning before I left the house, that I would rebuke Satan in the name of the Lord! Every day, I was going out there in a place with a lot of violence! When you go into Downtown Dallas, you would see the ambulance pull itself out every day. Then they would have the police all around the area.

When it came to Bible study, I had my plan figured out. I made a thing about young men and women. I had written my whole plan on notebook paper and put it all together. I made a thing called Problems of Young Men and Women.

I put ten things on paper. Times were bad; there was still killings going on with children. Times were bad and people just really don't know what to do. I had questions about one question. That question is: why do people have low self-esteem today?

They don't have the vision of God. That is one of the problems I put down. (I could tell you all ten but I will not.) I got ready for the next day. I got up in the morning to get ready for the next day.

I went back to the school. In the morning, it was the usual; you have Life Skills, Word of God, and prayer. We would have Life Skills every morning. He was still talking about the country.

He said this country needs help. People need to all just come together and figure out what needs to be done. We would not be so much in a struggle if we just worked together, rather than working by and trying to do everything ourselves.

We would be doing better than what we are doing. When I heard what he said, it was inspiring. Hearing someone talk about this country just had me thinking. I just don't know what to say about it. It was just something else when you hear people talk about this country.

Are they telling the truth about everything that is going on? I listened to what he said and I did not agree with it. This is the greatest country you are talking about. I could not hear it or see it at all.

I am one of those pulling for The United States of America all the time. Since I was hearing, seeing, and realizing all of this, I am going to say that this was just the beginning!

After all those years of slavery, all of the violence, and all of the hatred, this is just the beginning. I was realizing that after all the tragedies that were going on all around. I just could not believe in all the foolishness that was going on.

If this whole world was saved by the Lord and Savior, we would not be going through all of this, but the whole world was not saved by the Lord and Savior. You just had to pray for everything that was going on. Pray about everything. Hearing so much from my teacher, I just told myself, "I cannot believe in this. How could this be?" Well, it was all the truth. I could just accept the truth the way it was. Going from home to school, I could not believe in all of the foolishness that was going on. As I was going home, I was thinking about doing my thing that I had. I was getting everything together while I thought about doing it.

I had gone to Bible study, but no one was there except the bible study teacher, the woman that was praying for this nation, and another woman, and myself. We started Bible study with just a few of us.

We still talked about condemnation. After we got through with that, I explained what I was going to do. Everyone liked the idea. Then, I got myself together, and put out all of my things at Bible study. After that, the people called me a witness of God.

I did not know what a witness was at the time, so I looked it up in the Holy Bible. In the Holy Bible in Isaiah 55:4, it says, "Given him for a witness to the people, a leader and commander to the people." Here I go, getting ready to do my thing.

I was trying to let people know what was going on. Everyone liked my idea, so they told me to bring it in. I had to do something to do what I needed to do. I had written papers, typed papers, and printed out papers to do what I needed to do.

CHAPTER 6

IN THE TIMES OF THE DAY

In the quiet times of the day, I would get my things ready for Bible study. To be ready to do my thing, I had to get everything together. I had some ideas people loved. They just could not wait till I got my thing ready.

In the meantime, I was still going to the Training Academy. I would go there every week. We would do the same thing every morning. We would have Life Skills, the Word of God, and then prayer. Today, he had the talk again.

He was saying we are starting to put down one another, not loving one another as it says in the Bible. We put down one another, and then take away everything from each other till we have nothing in our lives. That is how bad it was in this country today. He talked about the country all the time. I could not help it but to just sit down and listen to what he said.

He knew mostly everything about the Democratic and the Republicans. I used to get taught that stuff in high school, but I had forgotten all about that stuff. That was what was going on, and he knew all about that stuff. He talked about that stuff all the time. Hearing from him was just hearing the truth. I used to ask my mother why everyone is not into the same thing. She told me, "Different strokes from different folks." I said, "What?" She said yeah. I said ugh. Then I said, "Different strokes for different folks." If we all had the same strokes it would be well, but we don't so keep on dreaming.

When I heard my mother say that, I thought of Gary Coleman's television show, "Different Strokes." It was something else in this country, but I was always thinking of the good times. I try not to hear about the negative.

I always try to hear the positive. There is always something going on, but I don't try to hear it. I always keep my mind on the positive times. The best times in this country are the good times. That is always the times I am trying to hear.

When the next week popped up, I got my things ready for Bible study. I got all my papers and stuff ready for Tuesday. Remember the time when I told you about the seven year old had got shot up in the car wash? The mother had come to church for prayer.

I walked out the door. I did not want to do it, but God said to do it! I headed back to the door. The light had come on. I had the light off. It was like God was telling me to go ahead and do what you want to do. I had walked out the door to the church.

I had everything that I was going to do on my mind at the time. I went to the church, and had my thing all ready. I went in and said hello to everyone. The Bible study teacher had explained everything. Then, I got started as soon as possible.

The first thing we did was my idea of the Problems of Young Men and Women. I stood up and explained what I was going to do. I talked to everyone about the Problems of Young Men and Women. I stood up and said my ten points. My ten points were:

1) They don't have the vision of God. They don't have anyone in their life that goes by God ways.
2) They have not accepted Jesus Christ as their Lord and Savior.
3) They are ungrateful. They are not considerate.
4) They are unethical. They are not making responsible choices and the right decisions.
5) They are hearing, seeing, and doing things in the Flesh of Law of Sin.
6) They are making themselves wise without the right knowledge.
7) They are insensible with others.
8) They are dealing with others in unethical ways.
9) They have low self-esteem.
10) They are not comfortable in church, so therefore they are not in or around church.

I had given all of my ten points. They loved it! They told me it was a good idea to do them. I said thank you. We talked about the ten points. We explained three points. That was it. I had done my idea and we had moved on.

The mother whose child got shot up in the school was there. She was reaching for prayer about what happened to her child. People could not believe what had happened to her child. They said that was terrible and just went straight to prayer.

I remembered when my parents told me about it. I could not think about someone doing a thing like that. I just don't know how you do it. My teacher had told me once, "Some people that do terrible things don't have feelings when they have done something terrible."

She was talking about when someone kills, beats, rapes, or hurts someone anyhow. Some people just don't have the feeling when they do crimes. I say you just have to pray for this country that we are living in. It is terrible how someone can take a baby or innocent child and just kill them.

Too many people in this country are in too much violence. Hearing and reading about all these tragedies in the news and the paper has to come to an end. It will all end when we see the Lord Jesus Christ. We have to pray every day. Sometimes life is war and every day is a battle you have to fight.

Just pray every day to keep your courage and faith up. That is what we have to do. I am just keeping my head straight and staying on the right path, walking in the Spirit of the Lord! I am doing things according to the Word of God!

It's hard to keep joy in our lives. God doesn't want to see us struggle. He wants the best for us. He loves everyone and we have to love one another. Most of us are God's children! We are just waiting to see ourselves one day come face to face with Jesus Christ in our lifetime!

We should have happiness in our lives because Jesus Christ never leaves us or forsakes us. His love is just amazing. There is no other love like God's love. His love is everlasting. Keep your hands in the Lord's hands. I have to go to church like my mother raised me to do. It is a good thing, not only for me, but for my family. Blessed be the angles that are protecting us.

This country is full of violence, hatred, killing, stealing, and jealousy. How can you just keep doing what is wrong, and not realizing what is right. It says in Isaiah 55:2, "Wherefore do ye spend money for that which is not bread and your labor for that which satisfies not? Hearken diligently unto me, and eat ye that which is good and let your soul delight itself in fatness."

Realizing what is good, and doing what is right is great. Faith, hope, peace, and love are what we need to make it in this life that we are in. To take a little blessing and turn it into something is a blessing. It says in the Bible, "Better is little with the fear of the Lord than great treasure and the trouble therewith!" Having the Lord on your side, all things are possible. Praise and worship him every day of your life! I was in church every day just to lift up the name of Jesus! I was building up my courage and strength, so I could continue walking through the days.

I had been going to the training academy. It was only a six weeks training course, and then you graduate. I had been talking to the teacher. He was still talking about the country. I told him there had been a whole lot of killings of children. He said there had been a whole lot of killings of everyone.

I said that there was too much killing of everything. I said, "Man, I cannot believe this." Most of the days, I had been talking about the country. With all of the hatred, violence, jealousy, and killing going on in this country, you really cannot depend on anybody else around you.

You just have to trust in God. You have to have faith and hope walking in the days of tragedy! Crisis! The country is filled with violence! You have to be strong. You have to have power and strength in your body. It is a tough world we are in. Every day is a battle you have to fight. I'd rather die as a fighter because there is no telling what would happen.

As I was moving on, I was worried about if I was going to graduate. I started thinking that I was not going to graduate from the training academy. I was thinking I was going to drop from the school. At the time, I had people telling me I was going to graduate.

While I was going to school getting ready to graduate, my aunt was telling me about the country, just like my teacher was telling me. She said this country has so many

problems. She said not too many people are willing to do what they need to do. She said that people need to do what they are supposed to do.

People out there are not doing what they are supposed to do, like I said last time! There are some people that would pretend to do something to help you. Then, they would take your money and go do other things with it. It is just too much going on in this country.

There is nobody that can really do anything to help us in these times. That is why you have so many people waiting on the Lord to come. All of us have to pray for this country, with the way it is going, but all prayers have to be for you to make it. If I had a whole lot of job opportunities, I would be better these days, but there are not a lot of jobs.

I was looking at the news. They wanted the president to make new jobs. There are so many people that need jobs. Some people are becoming homeless because they don't have jobs. Michael Jackson did a song called "Heal the World." That is what we need, healing in this world.

God is willing to do it if we just obey him. In a song called "Time to Get It Together," it says that Jesus Christ will heal all wounds. We have to live right to get the time-that's a Marvin Gaye song. That's one of my favorite songs.

It's deep down there in Downtown Dallas. They have violence, fighting, hating, and jealousy all down the area. You have to be all riled up with courage. If you don't keep your head up, you are going to get beat up down there.

I had one boy thinking he was going to do something to me. I had got my bag and got up, trying to go up to the front of the train. I walked by the boy with my bag. He pulls up his arms in a defensive boxing form. He said he was about to get my bag, but if I would have hit him, he would have tripped on me.

He looked at me thinking he was going to hit me. Then, he saw how much bigger I was than he was. In his mind, he must have said no. My aunt said there are too many young people without a purpose. They are here for a purpose. God put everybody here for a purpose, but then some are not doing their purpose.

I am doing well. Sometimes I feel like I am doing my purpose. They tell me to just keep doing what I am doing, and I will make it. With faith and hope, everything will come together in a good way. Having good things going on in my life is just what I need. If I just hold on, move forward, and stay strong in the days of tragedy, it will go fine.

I was still going to Bible study during the day. I had made a prayer request-I wanted to pray that I do well in what the Lord wants me to do. Someone said that you are doing a great job in your ministries. I told her thank you as we prayed. The child that got shot up in the car wash was a tragedy. I am not sure if it was one of the tragedies from where I was from, but it is a tragedy. It is something else. Just having children get killed is a terrible thing.

Coming to church was a good thing for her, so she could get all the prayers she needed. One time I was sort of down. Then, I went to church. When I got to the church, I was leaning to the side with tears coming down my eyes, just happy I had made it on the first day of church.

With the enemy trying to bring me down, I was crying because I had made it to church, where I could get prayer for my problems. I had times where Satan and the enemy were trying to put me down. It says in the Bible, "I will sit you at my right hand and make your enemies humble. Then, I will make them your footstool."

It is a battle every day when you get into the deep areas trying to make it. You see everything that is going on out there. There is too much violence going on in this country! When you go out in the deep areas, you see all the violence, hatred, jealousy, fighting, killing, and everything else that is going on. You have to pray for one another. You cannot just pray for yourself.

You have to pray for other people, too. You cannot just come in this world for yourself. We are around other people, too. It is all about God. We all have a purpose in life. We are all here for a purpose. I just pray to the Lord that I keep going on the right path in life. That is the main thing I pray for.

When I was going to the training academy, one of the owners told me I was in the last days of school. Finally, I was getting ready to graduate, but everyone had been telling me I was going to graduate. I was happy that I was getting ready to graduate. It was time to move on. I had been thinking negative, talking negative, and thinking I was not going to graduate, but I was going to graduate, and that was a good thing for me.

I had gone back on the train and I met someone as I was going home. She asked me was I working. I told her no, I was going to school. I told her I that was getting ready to graduate. Then, I told her that I had to take a test before I graduated. She told me that I was going to pass the test and graduate. I said thank you and moved on.

During the day, I had told my family I was going to graduate. My mother and father said that we were going to throw a party with the family. I thought about going to Taco Cabana, but my father said that will cost them money. Then, we had an idea to just have a cook out on the grill. I said all right! Then, we went ahead with that idea. A few weeks later, I graduated. The day after, we had a party!

Most of my aunts and cousins came over for the party. My mother bought me a custom made cake that said "Congratulations Franklon." I got another custom made cake. It was a butter finger chocolate cake.

We all had fun and a good time that day. We moved on through the day and let the good times roll. That's a rock n' roll song Jimi Hendrix made. I bought out Jimi Hendrix's "Electric Lady Land" and "The Godfather" that night.

My sister gave me an American Legend book that day. I was full of joy that day when the good times were rolling. I went back to the school. They said they would like to train me some more, so I let them. I was still going to school to get some more training in.

The school really wanted to work with me, so I let them keep working with me. Everything was going good for me at the time. The government was not making up any more lies about me. I was at a place where the owners are Christians. I had it good. I just needed to keep doing what I was doing, and I would make it without any problems. Having to wake up in the morning to make it to school was good. It was a good thing for me to do! Hearing my teacher talking about the country was me just hearing the truth! I was just trying to see through the rest of the days so that I would stay on the right path.

Hearing about this country is just the truth. It is time to get it together. Let's pray that God will bless The United States of America. "Jesus Christ, just Heal the World in these days of crisis!"

In the days of crisis and the days of tragedy, I can do all things that Christ who strengthens me. I started planning for the good things ahead in my lifetime! I wanted the best for myself, and at the time, to stay on the right path. I had faith and hope all whirled up in me.

As I was staying strong, moving forward, and holding on, I was making my way back and forth! I would just pull myself up where I would continue to seek the Lord Jesus Christ. The truth is what I needed to hear and see.

The Word of God is what I need. Ye shall know the truth. Then the truth shall set you free. As I continue going to church, I pray that my Spirit is filled with the Word of God. I will just keep striking as I am moving strong.

I will just keep fighting like I am doing. Then, I will make it out in this world of disaster. I will just keep going to the altar at church getting prayer. I am keeping myself ahead in the time, walking with courage in my mind. I am seeking the Lord with all my heart and with all my soul! I am staying in church, so therefore I am staying on the right path. I will just keep moving, holding on, and staying strong, all while I am praising the Lord Jesus Christ!

When I was at Bible study, I thought about doing more things, but I put it to the end. I stopped doing what I was doing. I thought it was not what the Lord wanted me to do! I just kept going to church. I would go to Bible study every week on Tuesday.

I would also go to church every Sunday. We saw the lady whose child was killed for the last time. Then, she stopped showing up at church. She was trying to get prayer for her child. Terrible things are going on in this country. It all needs to be put to an end.

That is why we have heroes. We have heroes for a reason till Jesus Christ comes back to save us. We are waiting till the day to the Lord comes. We have so many prayers for this country! One day, the Lord will heal the world. The Lord will come and restore the earth the way he had it.

Keep lifting up the name of Jesus, being of good courage and being of good cheer, as it says in the Bible. You have to keep your head up and your head straight, if you want to make it in the deep areas of Dallas and other cities. All over this country you have places that have non-stop violence. I am out here trying to make it. Pray for the places that we are in.

Most of our heroes have been killed in the crisis that we are trying to save. How do you feel about this? What's going on? Are the times changing for the good or the bad? There is no telling what is happening. Is there any hero willing to step up to save this place that we are living in? All of our heroes have died trying to save us.

Why don't we try to help fight back, like a soul brother with soul power! I can only keep my head up and my head straight in this foolishness-in the days of tragedy!

CHAPTER 7

GOING ON AS THE DAYS
ARE FLYING BY

Listening to the sweet, old music, I felt like I was flowing with the sweet old music! I used to drink beer till my sister and teacher told me to stop. I was at the park drinking a thirty-two ounce Budweiser. I was almost drunk.

Then, I felt the spirit of the Lord flowing over me, saying, "Why are you doing this?" He told me, "You can be anything you want to be." Then, I went home. When I got home, my mother told me I do not need to drink too much beer at night, before I take my medication.

It was not good for me to drink that much beer. They told me to quit, so I quit. My teacher said, "How much beer you drink is how much you are hurting your mother." He told me I needed to quit that. I did not want to do anything to hurt my mother, so I quit. I had hurt my father in a way, but not my mother. I was still going to the training academy to get some training in. I had stopped doing my thing at the church. I had stopped going in to most of the Bible studies.

When I stopped doing my thing at Bible study, most of the people had quit showing up at church. All of the people that were there when I was there had quit showing up at church. I was walking in the spirit of the Lord in my lifetime. The only thing that was wrong was that I was drinking too much beer.

All that drinking I was doing was hurting my mother, so I put it to a stop. My teacher asked me, "How are you going to be a Christian with all that drinking you are doing?" He said it was hard to say you are a Christian doing all that stuff. I was trying to continue walking in the spirit of the Lord in my life!

If we walk in the spirit, we shall also live in the spirit! I hope that one day, when I die, I will see Jesus Christ face to face! I am not alone, for God has said he will never leave us or forsake us. I am not afraid as I walk into the deep city. I'm walking in the spirit of the Lord to enter the presence of the Lord!

I shall not have the spirit of fear, for I am walking with the Lord with his rod. All of my beliefs are in the Lord. With my Father, we should have hope, peace, love, and diligence for and love one another to make it a better place!

We should try to bring a lot of love into our homes, community, family, and other places to reach others in a better way. I will keep myself moving strong to stop anybody from trying to pull me down from where I am today. Having faith is how I am going to make it. Hope says I will make it and faith says I will go for it.

Having faith builds up your confidence and it will also make you a stronger person.

That is always a reason a preacher talks about faith. It will make a better person out you. I pray that my days will be better than what they are. I will mostly get it.

How I would get faith is by reading the Word of God. Every day, I would go to the school, and talk about the Word of God. It's hard fighting the battle every day in your mind! I was hardly making it to Bible study, and the killing of innocent people in Arizona had been reported.

We would all get together at Bible study and just pray for the people, as the whole country with the president did! I would hop on and off the train, seeing, hearing, and witnessing what was going on around the areas where I was going.

All of the negative stuff was coming from the devil, and people were just letting the devil take control of them. The devil will put all types of thoughts in your mind. That is what the devil is doing to these people today. Going on the train, all of that stuff I saw is controlled by the devil somehow.

The young ones just don't have anybody to tell them about God. They cannot just figure it out by themselves. They need someone to help them figure it out. Those young ones are smart. They are not dumb. They are not like I was when I was with my group of friends.

If my friends and I were still together, we would be in jail right about now. The young ones were not that bad, except for the kids that went to school. They were so bad that I didn't even think they were school kids. Every day they got on the train and bus, they were doing something bad.

They were fighting, cursing, yelling, or screaming every day on the bus or train. The police would have to pull them off the bus and train because how bad they were acting. When you go out there in the deep areas, those young ones have not been taught how to act.

When you act so bad that you are not able to control yourself, it is a shame. There is something in the Bible you have to have: self control. You need to plead the Flesh and Blood of Jesus Christ over them. You are mainly doing it for yourself thinking how bad times are.

People were trying to take care of themselves. In these days, we are in a crisis. God Bless America and what we are going through. Times are hard, and I say we are at the very first beginning of bad times. Most of the time during the day, you want to cry.

Some people want to quit. It gets so bad, people kill themselves. Things are not going right for the United States of America. That's why I say God Bless America. We all go through trials and tribulations, but this is not necessary. Like the great African-American hero Malcolm X said, "All bad things end by any means necessary."

I wish our great heroes were still alive today. They killed most of our heroes. I still live by what they fought for and what they speak of and say. I do not look at anybody else but our great heroes.

I think we would not be going through this if they were still alive. Most of the stuff happening to me is because our heroes are dead! I get mad sometimes when I'm just sitting down looking at television facing the fact that they are dead!

Some of the terrible things that happened back then are happening today! If you look at the news, sometimes you will see a young innocent black man getting beat up by the cops for no reason. There are some things from back then that are still around.

They still have places for whites only around areas. Racism is still around. Just because your days have gotten better does not mean it is not around. Racism is being taught, and it is all around you.

Sometimes I think that things are not going to get better. My teacher told me once that things are not going to get better, and I have been thinking the same thing. What he said is probably true. You might as well go on with it.

If you cannot realize what is good, it is hard for you to stay on the right path. You have to realize what is good if you want to do well. One thing I pray for is that my crown be made of gold, rather than silver. That was a thing in the Bible-you getting awarded your crown in heaven.

I will put my soul and heart into the Lord and do everything according to his word forever and ever. Jesus Christ is the King of Glory, putting joy in my life. That is one reason I love him. I always put him first, before anyone else. I trust nobody but him.

When I was in Dallas, Texas, the changes started to come. I started to trust other people. As I was going through these places, I was praying for other people. I met this one guy that came home from the army. Every now and then, I would say a prayer for him.

We have to pray for one another in this world we are in. We have to love one another. God loves us all and we have to keep Him first. Jesus Christ died for to take away our evil ways. That is the greatest miracle of all miracles.

If everyone accepted Jesus Christ as Lord and Savior, this place would be better than what you think it would be. Seeing so much negativity in this place will have you thinking wrong. As I am trying to make it, I will say prayers that say, "Satan, get under my foot stool."

I will rebuke Satan; therefore I will have a good mind, body, and soul. Going into this world, you have to be with God. The Almighty God has power and authority over all.

Life is hard and there are times when it is not easy. My pastor has said, "You are going to go through trials and tribulations, but you still have to help yourself make it." I try to pull myself up and think positive in my life, especially when times get bad! I always try to keep a positive attitude. It is best when I get on my knees rebuking Satan and telling him to get under my foot stool.

Everyone needs God in their life. It is so bad going into Downtown Dallas, that these young guys robbed an elderly woman for her purse! Those types of guys that lounge their pants and have some types of problems in their life just need to be helped somehow.

Some of those guys are into violence, guns, drugs, and hatred on one another. It could all come to an end if they would just get saved and make changes in their lives. Going on, as the days are flying by, I usually watch who I run into. I do not want to start any trouble with these types of people.

Most of these people do not know how to take care of themselves. Those types of people were not taught anything while they were younger. You have to pray for one another while you are out here in this world. There are all types of things out here to kill us and destroy us. We have to believe in one another as we are helping each other.

A teacher told me that faith is what we have to go by. Seeing the places where people have trials and tribulations, I just wish I could help them out. I am only one man trying to make it, and the only thing I can do is pray.

I hear the sweet old music! I feel like I am flowing through the music. It's probably just me. I don't think anybody else has that type of feeling. If someone does, I am wrong. Having to see all of this, I just really feel terrible about it! I do not know what it is, but it needs to come to an end.

Seeing all of the young ones' hatred for one another is just terrible. Why so much hatred on one another, when you can love one another like the Bible says? Maybe people are not hearing the Word of God. The whole world will fall apart if you are not hearing the word.

We live by the Word of God. That is how we make it every day. You have to hear the word and study it. If you do not study, you will not know. They say it is hard to be a Christian. It is hard to be a Christian these days.

With the way things are going in life, I guess there is as much going negative as there is positive. I just pray sometimes that everything would go right. Then I pray I will make it out of this cruel world. I do not even try to put myself with the world. I would just keep myself in Christ's name. This world has so much going on that you do not need the negative in your life! This world has a lot of evil going on. Most of our problems are caused from the evil of the world. Most of this stuff I see is from the world.

When I start to see all this stuff, I think it is from other people. Then, you have the world with its ways. It might not be who you think it is. Most of this stuff is from Satan. You have to keep your eyes on God to stay on the right path.

I hope that the days get better while we are living the life we are in today. As I am going on, my mind stays positive with positive thoughts. All my faith was in what I was doing. I was going to school trying to make it, waiting for the time to just come to me.

When the time comes, it will just come. I have to be in the time of the days! I'm always wishing that things would be better for when I move on. Seeing myself in the time of the days, those things will get better when I move on. Some days I have to pray for myself.

All the days I will rejoice in the name of the Lord and hope I will see greater days in my life. Tragedies are occurring in most of our lives. Sometimes we do not know what to do about it. Life is hard and I think we all struggle to make it through.

Struggling is the difficult part. Most of us struggle. We have our heads down, thinking that we not going to make it. We are more than conquerors. We have to keep our heads up, stay positive, think positive, and just keep going. There is nothing else we can do but have faith in ourselves.

In most of our lives, we have struggles. We have to keep our head up to make it. As I move on in these days, I will continue to move strong. I'm moving strong, holding on, and going forward. It is a battlefield everyday when you step outside.

I will continue walking in the Spirit of the Lord while my enemies are trying to bring me down. The Lord will sit you at his right hand. Then, he will make your enemies humble and make them your foot stool. You have to have power and strength to make it in these days.

Your mind has to be filled with courage. As you are filled by the spirit with the Word of God, do all the things according to the Word of God. You will be fine in the times of the day. Just take diligent heed of his commandments and law!

Love your Lord God! The Lord has charged you to cleave unto him, and to serve him with all your heart and soul. Love your God Jesus Christ!

Is that what you are really supposed to do, just keep your faith and your hope alive? Is that what we have to do out here in this world? Getting up early in the morning is hard, but it is worth it every minute.

Moving forward and moving on, I will continue to strive to make it. There are so many problems that are confusing. We just do not know how to handle it. The best thing to do is let God handle it.

Just keep moving forward in life. I will continue to make it and do what I need to do, while forcing myself just a little bit. I will continue to live by faith as I am doing now. Seeking the Lord, I will continue to praise and worship his holy name.

As we are in the days of the tragedy, we have to depend on God to make it. We are all going to have struggles, but we are more than conquerors. We will win the battle that we are going through. We go through trials and tribulations, but God is going to work everything out.

There is a Word of God in the Holy Bible. It says "let there be peace during the storm." God will take all of your problems away. Just trust in God! Jesus will work everything out if you just trust in him. I will continue to praise and worship Jesus Christ as I am walking in these types of days! These days, there is all types of chaos going on, and there is hardly any people that are willing to put it to an end.

During these times, we are looking for somebody else to save us! We need to look up to the Lord and Savior Jesus Christ to put all of this foolishness to an end. All of my faith, hope, peace and love will go onto the Lord. He is my one and only father and I will forever love and look upon Him.

I'm putting all of my trust in His holy name! I hope that I will see Him face to face one of these days. I just cannot wait to see the Lord. The place where we are going to see Him will be better than this place we are in today.

We are in an evil world today. I do not agree with this today. I do not make myself a part of the world of today. I keep myself lined up with Jesus Christ. I agree with Jesus, not with this foolishness that we are having in this world today.

I do not try to mix myself with this foolishness that is going on today. I just try to keep my head straight and keep moving strong in life. You have to be strong in this world today. I just hope I make it.

While I am going through my trials and tribulations, they said, "Let there be peace during the storm," so let there be peace. He is the King of Glory, putting joy in my life. I have hope and faith that I will make it.

Keeping my head straight, I am moving strong as I walk in the days of the struggle. As I go out there, I see people that need to be helped. I just pray for myself as I am moving through the days. It is hard just to go out there and see the things I would see every day.

There is nobody willing to end it. I hope that things to come to an end and that we will get things going right. I see this country in a struggle as my teacher talks about it every day. There is somebody willing to put it to the end.

As I continue to walk forward, I will continue to keep my head straight. I will continue to move strong as I am moving on. I pray that I will continue to be on the right path and that I will make it out of this world that I am in today.

Thank you, Jesus, for protecting me in this time of the day! Bless the angels that are looking over me. I have the Holy Spirit guiding me and directing me onto the right path in life. As I move strong in this lifetime, the days will continue to get tougher, so I will just pray for myself.

CHAPTER 8

Moving Strong

As I am keeping my head straight and moving strong in the days of struggle, I will continue walking in the spirit of the Lord. I put all of my faith and hope into the Lord! I just pray that I will make it during these times. These are tough times and I will continue praising the Lord.

As I was walking on in the days, I started to miss the days of training. I went to the park to walk around. As I walked around, I saw an old guy reading the Holy Bible. He had a computer listening to Christian music. I walked by, and then I said, "Would you like a 'Jesus Loves You' card?" He said, "I sure would like one!" I asked him if he comes to the park often. He said yes. I said nothing then.

He said, "I can remember meeting you. You look like someone I know." I said I was not sure. He asked me what my name was. I said, "My name is Franklon."

He said, "I know you! I met you at the park before. It has been a while." He told me his name, and I remembered. I said it had been a while.

We talked for a while. Then, as we kept talking, I asked him, "Would you like to pray together." He said yes! Then we sat by each other at the park, took each other's hand, and started to pray at the beautiful park.

It felt good when we prayed together. I really don't know him well, but he was a good, Christian man. They say when two Christian people come together in the midst and give God all the glory, it is a great thing.

The blacks in the days of slavery would always come together. They would pray to God about what they are going through. The blacks in slavery always depended on God. These days, I am not too sure about blacks. The blacks in the slavery days were wiser than blacks today. I just have to pray for myself as I am moving strong in these days.

The people in Jesus Christ's days would even pray together as they were moving on. Most of us these days would not pray together. It would be a whole lot better if we all got together and prayed. I have the dream of people praying together! I just get happy when people just pray together, especially when you meet other Christians that you do not know! It just feels good when you do.

As I was moving along, I thought about people praying together. I would go home hoping that I would see more people and pray some more. I was just hoping to do good as I was moving on. I was taking a step forward in my life, which would help me accomplish what I was trying to do. I had hope moving forward that my dreams and goals would be a success. I just had to keep my faith up! As long I had faith, I would have accomplishments and successes, and I could overcome anything that I was doing.

Going to school was a good thing for me. The only bad thing was that I had to get up early in the morning to catch the train. It was a good school. It was a good place to go to if you were trying to make it. It was tough going down in that area. There were all kinds of things going on as you were going to those places. You would see all types of things going on as you were moving in those deep areas. One of the main things you would see was homeless people. I had a bad feeling when I saw a homeless person. I could not see how you could be homeless with storms and all types of things going on outside. I also saw opossums and rats outside! They had all of that going on outside. People were homeless, and all of that was going on outside where they were. Being homeless was not anything good. That's why there are people out there trying to help.

My mother told me that the reason some people were homeless was because they were into too many drugs. I did not like the idea of being homeless. Being homeless is just not a good thing. Most people that are on drugs are not saved. Most of those people have not accepted Jesus Christ as Lord and Savior.

When you accept Jesus as the Lord and Savior, he will take away all of your problems. He will give you eternal life. His love is everlasting. His mercy, grace, and Wondrous Works of God are a blessing. You need to know that he will never leave you or forsake you!

I see young men and women lounging their pants, fighting, cursing, and not loving one another! What is going on? Too much chaos is happening around me. There is no one out there really trying to help this issue.

All the hatred going on needs to be put to an end. Satan is controlling some of these young ones' lives out here. All of these things are wrong and hatred is not the answer. All of the jealousy, hatred, violence, and fighting will not solve the problems.

With so much going on out here, you just have to pray for people out here in these areas. Too much foolishness is going on. What's going on out here in the world today? I know something is going on, looking at the news on television and in the newspaper! I quit looking at the news trying to get away from all of tragedies that are going on.

When are people going to try to make a change? There are too many people with power not doing anything about it. It just makes me mad sometimes seeing people with a lot of power do nothing. It is like not doing your job or what is right.

You are not getting away because you are in the world with everything going on. The only time it will end is when we all go to heaven-the Kingdom of God! I just cannot wait to make it to heaven. Home Sweet Home is what that is.

Everything is perfect there with Jesus Christ. All of my faith and hope goes into the Lord. I thank Jesus for dying on the cross to take us away from our evil ways. I am trying to get away from the evil, but I am right in the middle of it just by getting on the train, witnessing all of these problems!

As much as I want to get away, the closer I get, the more involved I am. I am trying to get away, but I have to be in these same places that I am in. I would just like to make a wish and throw a quarter into a wishing well. If I could, I would wish to get away from all of this foolishness! When I see myself in these types of days, I just pray for myself.

I would still pray for others, like the Bible says, but I believe in praying for myself, too. I would pray for others to have faith in and believe in one another! I have faith in myself and I believe that I will make it. At one time, I would not pray for someone else or believe in someone else. I would try to do everything for myself rather than for someone else. Then one day, I decided to pray for someone else.

When I was on the train, I saw a soldier coming home from the army. He was a black man who was coming home to see his family. I saw people talking to him. Then, I went up to him and asked him, "Are you in the army?" He said yes, so I asked him for his name. He said his name is Neo. I told him I would pray for him. When I got off at my stop, I had told him, "I will pray for you again, one more time." Then I left and went home. That is one of the first times I prayed for someone else. I usually would have not prayed for anyone else. It says in the Holy Bible to pray for and love one another. I guess when I started, I had someone praying for me and loving me also. I guess the love had started to come from people. I know, and then I don't know.

Back then, we had money problems, and we could not afford the expensive things. I did not have custom made cakes and fancy things, like other kids. I usually just had the cakes made for a dollar, and that usually was my birthday cake. Not all of those fancy customs made cakes cost a lot of money. I was thinking it was so cool for other people to have fancy things.

I was always raised up where we had struggles, like trying to fit in with your friends because they had brand new video game systems. It was all good with my friends because I was the coolest guy to hang with. When my birthday came around, all my friends would come over to party and hang out at my house. They would even give me birthday gifts. I remember those times that I used to have. It may be the struggle, but there were good times in those days! I will always remember those days, doing things like having to walk outside with a hood over my head and wearing my favorite jeans every day!

I loved being on the basketball team for the school, talking about when I made it to the professionals, I would be rich. I remember those days. Those are some classic days. Those are the days I will never forget. I love just thinking about those days!

I remember one Christmas, I only got two things. It was a basketball and a CD player. I walked up and down the street with my basketball with my head down. Later on, I went to the gym with the basketball. We would play basketball at the gym all day and night till it closed.

One day, it was stolen and that was the end of that. That Christmas was the best Christmas I had ever had. That is one Christmas that I will never forget. When I think about it sometimes, I feel like I hate myself because I was not that smart. If I was smart, I would have had my head up, but I didn't. I just have to keep my head up and just keep moving strong. I'm holding on to life by the branches, hoping that I will make it in the name of the Lord. I can do all things through Jesus Christ, who strengthens me.

Seeing all of these things going out here, I just have to pray for that strong brother fighting for our lives in this country. The soldiers in the army are good men, and you have to give them credit for what they do. I had days where I wanted to be a soldier, but my mother told me not to do it. She made me think about not getting in the army. When I was younger, that was a dream I had. If I can pray for a soldier in the army, I can pray for anybody else. Once I prayed for the soldier, I had a mind to pray for other people. I started to pray for my friend, my neighbors, and then my family.

I was once thinking of myself, and then I started to think of others. I started to build up in my mind that I would start to give to other people. What I started doing was buying gift cards and putting the Word of God in it. Then, I would give it to people as a gift. That was one way I would start to give. I always thought that was one good way of giving. I put the Word of God on the card. Then, I would give them a card as a gift.

It was coming Christmas time, and I wanted to do something for somebody. I wanted to do something for my Bible study teacher. I did not have a lot of money or anything else. I had in mind to give her a Christmas card. I bought a Christmas card saying "Let's rejoice when Christ was born." It was the best Christmas card I had seen celebrating when Jesus Christ was born!

It is one of the best things to do, celebrating the day of the Lord and Savior! I bought the card and put a Word of God on it. I put a word out of Ezekiel on the card, "And the Lord said speak. Speak said of the Lord. Thus speak of the Lord. Speak of Israel every one come to you. Everyone in your mind!"

I said, "Let's keep our eyes on the Lord, so we can obey what he wants us to do." I gave her that card as a gift. She hugged me and thanked me for the card. That was the way I started to give, as I started to not think of myself and started to think of others.

I was walking on the path ways that I saw other men trying to pursue to the end! All of these things going on have to have somebody behind it. These young people are picking up other people's habits that have people talking about all of this pants lounging, cigar smoking, fighting, and hating going on.

These young ones are picking it up from other people. It is not hurting me, but it is probably hurting someone else. All of these things going on are from other people. It is like picking up a bad habit. I am praying for our heroes everyday to be blessed, trying to help our country. This country is just full of foolishness and evil.

We cannot stand to just be here on earth. You can either transform to a new creature, or conform to this world. After all that I am witnessing, I'd rather be transformed into a new creature. Jesus Christ said in the Holy Bible, "You have to be born again to enter the Kingdom Of God!"

I have been born again; therefore, I will not conform to this world. I will not try to align myself with the way the world goes. I will look to the Almighty God and his ways of perfection, not the way of the world with this foolishness. I will find all of the things that I am seeking!

People are talking about trying to fix problems every day. It will all end when we see Jesus face to face. I pray for myself as I walk in the spirit through the dark alleys and other places! I pray for myself every day that I will continue to seek the Lord!

I pray that the Lord will bless me as I am moving on in life! As I was moving in life, I used to read the Holy Bible. I would pick up the Holy Bible read, study, and memorize the scriptures. I was one with the Word of God! "And the Lord said. Speak said of the Lord. Thus speak of the Lord. Speak of Israel everyone will come to you. Everyone in your mind!"

I would speak of nothing but the Word of God, and nothing but the Lord Jesus Christ. I would speak it every morning when I would go to the training academy. It helped me to keep focused on God. That took away the negative times in my mind.

I had some things from back then that I would focus on all the time. I would get rid of those things when I was talking about the Word of God. Keeping my mind focused on God helped me feel better all the time. That was my way of getting out of things that I used to do, like getting up with the posse, going around the neighborhood.

Time to get it together! It is a battlefield in your mind, and the way I get my mind together is by speaking about the Word of God. I always feel better when I just speak the word every morning. That is my way of getting out of things.

There's so much evil, hatred, and violence going on out here! Some places are not places for people to go. I was out there in those places, and let me tell you that most of the people out there are not saved. Imagine if this whole world was saved today. Everybody would be getting fulfilled, not getting drunk off of beer and wine.

Everybody would love one another, care for one another, help one another, and even pray for one another. We would all pray together, believe in one another, and have faith in one another. It would not be like this with all of the tragedies that are going on. The world would be a better place if we were all saved.

All the things that are going on would be positive. Just have a dream and imagine if we were all saved. I just cannot wait till we all see Jesus Christ. Meeting him face to face will be a joyful moment, taking all the blessings that he is giving us!

Then, I would thank him for his mercy and grace. Thanking Jesus is a wonderful thing to do. It is a beautiful thing to be a Christian in life. Being a servant to the Lord Jesus Christ and to his people is a blessing!

It is a blessing to have the Holy Spirit, especially when you are around a bunch of people that have the Holy Spirit with them! It is a great thing to have. Once you feel the Holy Spirit, you just want it to stay with you forever. The feeling of the Holy Spirit is good, and you would never want it to leave you. With all of these things I am doing, the Holy Spirit guides me.

Walking out here in these deep areas, you are going to run into the wrong person. If you run into the wrong person and make the wrong decision, you will get yourself onto the wrong path in life. You especially do not want to run into a drug dealer that wants you to deal drugs with him.

If you go out with him, you are going to lose your family and your life. My teacher called North Dallas, where I used to live, a bad place. It might have been worse than I thought it was. It was probably one of the worst places, but the absolute worst place I knew was South Dallas. You would always hear about someone getting killed down there in that city. South Dallas would always be on the news.

As I am looking forward, I am expecting good things to happen in my life. Even with all the trials and tribulations, I am expecting the good times to happen. Let the good times roll! In this life we are living, I am looking for all the good times to happen. I am not looking for all the bad times. "Let the good times roll," like that good rock n' roll song Jimi Hendrix made. "Let the good times roll!" I just had to say it again! Think of the good instead of the bad times.

We should just have a heart full of joy! Putting a smile on our faces would make a whole lot of difference. Trust me, I know, because when I was younger, I would not smile at all. I would always do a mean look at you, and then I would say something mean to your face just to make you mad and to cause you to have a bad day. I used to do things like that. Just put a smile on your face! You would make your days a whole lot better.

There are all types of people in this world that would do all kinds of things to you! You do not know what you might run in to a day's time. You might run into people that will try to put you down every day of your life! You just need to get away from that person that is talking bad about you and tearing you apart on the inside. Look to and hope for your days to get better.

Just surround yourself with positive people, and watch things change in your life. All kinds of good things will happen if you just keep yourself positive. Do what's positive, think positive, act positive, and then you are positive. Things will fall into place.

You will see that time will fly by as the hard times are coming around. Time flies by faster every day, and I just wish it would go by slower. It is in the Bible to take one day at a time! That is one thing we have to do.

There is no telling what will happen in our days. Only God knows everything that is going to happen. I'm just keeping my head up and moving strong in the days, hoping and praying that the days get better. I am waiting till better days rise up in our lives!

I hope that one day, everything will be perfect, and we'll have the days of perfection! Everything God does is perfect. Seeing everything perfect in these days would be fine. Then again, everything will not be perfect, because no one's perfect. Jesus is the Great I Am and He is the only one who is perfect. God's love is everlasting and that is perfect. I love the mercy and grace of God!

Pray for this country we are in. All of these things that are going on need to be put to an end. Everything out here is getting worse and worse. It will have your mind thinking that things will not get any better. It is going to get better faster than you think. No one around here is the Lord and Savior, and it is going to get better. You just have to give it some time. It will come around eventually. You may not see it now, but you will see it later on. You have to have patience. Patience is in the Bible and that is one thing you have to have.

I used to have a lot of patience, but I think I lost some of it. In these times, there is a lot going on, and there are things that you might not know till someone tells you a year later. So much is going on and the only thing you can do is pray. I'm just holding on to the power and strength in my life, praying that I have the strength to make it every day. When I see what we are going through in this country, I know that we have a lot of work we have to do. Just bringing up all the problems people talk about every day is not helping. We are not working together to get things done in the meantime.

Like my teacher said one time, "If we can all work together as a country, we would be doing better than what we are doing now."

"The change is coming if we can just keep moving forward as we are doing." A guy that works for the school told me that.

When we do something that we are supposed to do, Satan will tempt us to stay where we are. We have to force ourselves everyday to take a step forward. I took a step forward by going to the training academy. I did not want to go, but I went to the school anyway. I got a certificate out of it. While I was moving forward, I was still expecting some more good times to come. I have to work for all the good times I want, just like I did when I was going to school to get an education.

When you get through with school, the time for celebrating comes. Having all of your family coming over to congratulate you, getting gift cards and gifts, receiving some money, and receiving a lot of hugs from your love ones; all of these things are a celebration. All those good times are times you remember. Those are the times when you should get the camera and take photos of yourself, your friends and family members.

You get all joyful when those times come around and you just become thankful to God when you are having a good time. Good times are always going to come around, so just be ready to put a smile on your face for the camera. Letting the good times roll is a favorite thing. Just have joy in your heart when you wake up in the morning and see the sunshine!

I thank God for waking me up every morning. I used to do it all the time, but then I fell off track. I just wish I could do it like I used to do. Then again, it might come back to me. It is a blessing, just thanking the Almighty God for waking me up every morning. It gives you joy in your heart when you thank Him. Have a blessed day in your life, knowing that all things will come together in Jesus Christ's name! With His authority in power over all, there is no search, nor counsel, or understanding greater than the Lord God.

God has all power, and there is nothing that can go against Him. I pray that one day we all will see Jesus! When we all go to heaven, we will all be with Him. He is with us now, as He gave us His word. He will never leave us or forsake us. We are already with Him.

We are just praying to see Him face to face. We shall behold His love and the blessings that He will give us in heaven. There is a reward for everyone when we make it to heaven. Not rewards like gifts from a man. God is not man. He is God of Gods. All things will come together by His glory. He is the King of Glory shining His light in our lives.

He is the light of the world. The light of the world is Almighty God. I just have to thank Him for the blessings in our lives and for allowing us to continue to seek Him! He loves all of us and wants the best for us in our lives. He loves us before we love Him.

He knew us before He even sent us to earth. I just feel terrible hearing that some people do not love the Lord. He loves all of us, so you should show some love back. Just pick up your Bible every now and then, and it will be good. He wants us to know Him real well, and we have a whole lot of studying to do.

We have to know the Word of God real well. Just to make us joyful in life, we have to pick up our Bible and do all the right things according to the Word of God! We will be alright. I pray that you and your family will have a blessed life. I pray every day that my day will be a blessed day, as well.

I am so thankful for what God does for me! I never have the thought of cursing at God. I do not blame anything on Jesus. I always blame myself for what I do in life. I put all of my blames on me, and not on my Father up above. He is worthy of everything, and we are His loving children.

We are God's children and He loves us with all His heart. Most people will not show Him love back. It is sad and makes me feel bad knowing He loves us all and there are people that don't love Him back. That is not good, but everyone does not know who Jesus Christ is.

I did not know who He was till somebody told me about Him. There was a young guy standing in front of a building trying to get people to know Jesus. He saw me walk by and talked to me for a while. He told me to read the book of Matthew. I turned my bible to Matthew. In the front, it said 'The New Testament.' It said Jesus Christ was the Lord and Savior. I was reading my bible after Exodus. I was barely getting into my Bible, and this guy came to me quick to tell me about Jesus.

Jesus Christ is the Bread of Life! I thank Him every day for His Wondrous Works. Bless his holy name. Bless him! I'm moving strong as I am walking in the spirit of the Lord, praying that I will get power and strength from being a child of God! To have the flesh and blood of Jesus Christ all over my body is a blessing!

Pleading the flesh and blood of Jesus Christ all over my body, I come in the spirit to do what the Lord wants me to do. He wants me to obey His commands. As I was moving on in the days, I would go to the park to read my Holy Bible. There was a beautiful park that I had gone to and prayed together with a guy I had not seen in a while. We would meet at the park and greet each other.

It was a blessing that children of God could come together. I had gone to the park to read my Holy Bible and sat down on a bench. There was a guy next to me on another bench. He had his head down holding a cross in his hands. I was looking at him wondering why he was looking sad. I took off my cross and said, "I have a cross, also."

I told him, "You have a nice cross." He told me it was some type of cross. I said that was nice. I said, "You have your head down, and you are looking pretty sad. Are you alright?" He said he was just having a down time. I asked him, "Would you like to pray together?" He lifted his head up with joy and said sure.

While he was looking real sad, I sat by him on the bench. We grabbed each other's hands. Then, the spirit got in us and we started to pray together. We prayed about twenty minutes. It was a good prayer. When I got through, I said, "Alright, it is done." We prayed together while he was having a bad time.

I went back to my bench. I told the guy, "May the Lord bless you." Five minutes later, he said thank you and lifted his head up. He quit looking sad all of a sudden. He got up with his head up straight and walked off strong and bold with a lot of power and strength.

He went home as a different person. When we prayed together, everything for that man changed. A change happened inside of him. Everything became different when we prayed. We prayed at the beautiful park and everything had changed when we did.

They say there's power in praying people. The guy really needed prayer. He said he was having a bad time. He was probably having a worse time then what I was thinking. Only God knows! I was just a person that God had sent to help that person. I had the feeling that God sent me.

I had been thinking that God was using me for a reason. He was using me for a perfect reason. He was using me for what I had prayed for. I had prayed for God to shine my light in other people's lives and let me be a blessing to others. He was doing that for me, but it was also a blessing for me.

I can be a blessing to other children of God as we come together in the midst and pray. Praying together is a beautiful thing to do. Have faith in our Lord Jesus Christ, as He has faith in us! We are His children and He loves us! Bless His holy name, as He is worthy. Magnify and sanctify Him, as He is the God of Gods. Lord, just bless yourself as you are doing your Wondrous Works. As we are the children of God, we shall continue seeking Him.

Continue to praise and worship Him. We have the blessing to be able to come together and pray with each other. It is a blessing to come together with other Christians you really don't know. It is great loving one another and praying for one another. We have the gift to be able to care for someone else!

It is always a blessing to be able to get together like the people did in the Bible. It was always a blessing when the people in the Bible got together.

Now, we do not get together like that at all. If we would get together like the people did in the Holy Bible, it would make a difference here in this country, but we are stuck just hating one another.

We are not getting along with one another. We are fighting each other, hating one another, getting jealous of each other, and killing each other. We have all of this violence in one country that is unnecessary. There's just a big whole bunch of foolishness that is going on. We just need to come together.

Too much sad stuff is going on. It is happening so much, and it seems like no one is doing their job. Most people are not doing what they are supposed to do, but some people are making sacrifices to help us. Our heroes are making sacrifices every day to help this country. Everybody just has to do what they need to do, and it will be alright.

We are facing challenges today. We are going through some challenges and we have to overcome them. We are fighting a battle every day to get where we want to be and get things how we want them to be. We want this place to be the best place ever. It will be if we can just get this place together.

We can still pick up the broken pieces and shattered dreams that we had. Eventually, we will be alright. Today, we are starting to see with our own eyes. The blessing of coming together has to be a blessing from God. That has to be a wonderful blessing from the Lord. God gives us gifts and we have to use those gifts.

There are so many people with great gifts from God, such as art, poems, music, and writing, which people are not using. People just have to use them so that they have a good gift that they can look at every now and then! You know if you have a blessing or not. You will continue to use it if you just keep moving forward. Keep taking a step forward and you will continually get blessed for what you are doing.

These days, we are in a struggle. We just have to hope that God will bless us. One day all of this foolishness will come to the end. All of the negativity that is going on is becoming worse. Why is all of this happening? Is it that people gave up trying and quit what they started? Is it that it is useless trying to fix it? All of these things going on out here need to be put to an end. All these tragedies are driving us crazy! There are so many crises in the United States of America-violence, killing, hatred and jealousy of one another! Can all of this be put to an end?

Will it come to an end, so we can put a smile on our faces today? We need hope, like in the book, "The Book of Hope," a Christian book written a long time ago. It is a small book telling us to have hope. It has some scriptures from the Bible in it. It is a good book to read. It will keep your mind focused on what you are doing.

I had another Christian book, but I forgot the name of it. It was a good book, too. It was small just like the other book that I was talking about. Some good books are small and need to be put into a big book, but that is the author's decision.

While I was going on and off the train, I was talking to my friend that I went to high school with. We had not seen each other for a while, so we had a plan to do something. We talked about this movie on television that looked good, so we decided to go see it. We went to the Cinemark Theater to see the movie, and it was good.

It was not everything my friend expected, but it was alright. He said there was not a lot of action. We planned to go to the bar after the movie, but I decided to go home. Everyone else was getting pretty tired, so they were happy I wanted to go home.

There was another guy that went with us to the movie. It was one of my friend's best friends. We had taken an extra person with us. It was a good time out.

I went to the movies another time. I saw my Godmother at the thrift store. I had not seen her since I was six years old. I was looking for something to wear to the movies. She came up to me and said, "Franklon?" I asked her who she was. She said that she was my Godmother. I asked her how she was doing, and she said that she was doing fine. She asked me, "What you are doing here?"

I said, "I am looking for something to wear to the movies." She asked me what movie I was going to see and I said, "The American". She said she did not like that movie because it had too much violence.

My favorite gangster action movie was "The Godfather," so of course I was going to see it. I went to see the movie theater and nobody was there. I was the only one in the movie theater. The whole movie theater was empty.

I went out to the parking lot and there was only a Mercedes out front. The movie was probably not good, like my Godmother said.

I kept all my tickets when I went to the movies. Sometimes, I would look back to see what movies I had gone to see. I had seen a lot of movies.

It wasn't the only movie that did not have anybody going to see it. There was nobody in the whole movie theater. It was empty. I enjoyed the movie. I hoped that it would come out on DVD. After I enjoyed that day, I talked to my friend. His other friend was having his birthday at a club. His birthday was coming up and they were going to celebrate.

He was going to have his birthday party at a comedy club. I was talking to my friend on the phone. He said I could come along because they had an extra ticket. I called back later on to make sure. He said they did have an extra ticket, so I got all dressed up for a night out.

At nine o'clock at night, we went to the comedy club. It was by the train station I go to every day. Everyone, including me, had a great time. It was really funny. It was one of the best times I had ever had. I really enjoyed the time out. I told everybody about my night out.

It was a good place to get out, have fun, and to meet new people. It was a nice little place to go. That was just what I needed. I used to always get out and meet new people just to take my mind off of things. I enjoyed the times out. I met some cool people when I got out. They were not my friends, but they were cool.

To me, when I would get out, it was all about the women with fancy cars. You know the women that wore those expensive high heels? I talked to some women like that. They were from Dallas, just like I was. They were just visiting the bar in Downtown Plano. I had only seen them that one time when they visited.

I did not have any money when I went to the bar. I would just go to the bar without money. I would have a good time even though I did not have any money. I would just go up there to talk to the women. When I would go up there without money, I would get some water and just throw darts near the bar.

The bar was always my hangout. I would always go in the daytime just to get out of the house. It was an everyday thing for me. I probably should not have made it an everyday thing, because I really needed to be working.

You have to work for everything you get. It is not easy in life. Life is not a joke. What a fool believes is probably that. Life is tough and you have to be strong, especially where I am from and with what I would see out in the cities where I lived. I saw all kinds of things in the type of places I was in and the places I would go to and by every day. There were hard times in those places at the time. It was too much negativity going around. I just needed to pray that those people would get saved.

It makes a difference when you have the Lord in your life. With the Lord and Savior, all things will come together in Jesus' name. The Lord will heal you with His Holy touch, and you will be healed by His stripes. We will have struggles in this life. We will have challenges, and we have plenty of days to overcome them. You will also have to overcome your enemy.

Satan and the enemy are here to bring you down with all of their plans. You have to destroy all their plans and put them down. You have to go to church and shout out in the church. I've gone to church and danced all in the front rows.

I did a dance once, and a lot of people talked about me. I was dancing, I tell you! Someone asked me what type of dancing I was doing. I told him I was doing the Holy Ghost dance! I was really just dancing up and down the aisle and it felt good. It is good just to praise and worship the Lord. I love going to church every Sunday and giving Him glory! What an awesome God we have. The Lord is my shepherd and I shall forever praise Him.

He loves me no matter what I do. He accepts the righteous and the unrighteous. We shall forever love Him for what He had done for us. Be joyful in life and just give God the glory. Thank you, Jesus, for blessing me to wake up every morning! He does not have to wake me up every morning, but He did because He loves me.

Just give Him the glory because He is the Great I Am. He is worthy of everything, and He has the power over all authority. As the days get tougher and the time gets harder, I just pray to have strength to make it through these times. I just wish things would get better in these times and I'm hoping that I will wake up by the sunshine every morning!

Faith, hope, peace, and love are the things I pray that I will have every day! God bless this country where we are trying to get things right. You have the saying 'wrong is right,' but you have to overcome that saying. You cannot be thinking that wrong is right. You know that The Lord Jesus Christ is sanctified in the righteousness.

Saying 'wrong is right' does not make any sense at all. Jesus is the most beautiful name. Just thank the Lord for what He has done. Tell the Lord to magnify and sanctify himself for His Wondrous Works. He says He will never leave you or forsake you. The Word of God is the truth. We have to hear the Word of God if we want to live a good life.

Pray for a blessing and you will get it. Just pray for what you want and you will eventually get it. Just pray for a blessing and you will feel a whole lot better. The Wondrous Works of God are a blessing in our lives. We just have to accept that blessing.

So many of us have gifts and we are just not using them. One gift that I love the most is giving. That is a true blessing to me, how a person just gives another person a gift. That is a blessing from God to me. Jesus has always loved people, even when He was mad one time. That is a real true blessing. It is more of a blessing to give than to receive. That is in the Holy Bible. To me, that is a blessing.

I am moving strong as I am in these days. I am walking strong in the spirit of the Lord. I continue to pray every day in the days of tragedy! I will continue praising and worshipping the Lord as He is doing His Wondrous Works. Give God all the glory for what He has done for us. He gives us power and strength in these days. He wakes us up in the morning to see the sunshine.

As I was walking strong in the spirit of the Lord, I went to the park one day. I was walking around and I saw a young black man reading his Holy Bible at the park. I asked him how he was doing. Then I said, "Are you reading your Holy Bible?" He said yes, so I asked him if he wanted to pray together. He said yes.

He said, "What do you want to pray about?" I told him what I wanted to pray for was to keep my eyes focused on the Lord and do everything according to the Word of God. He said that was fine. He told me to stand there and let's pray. He prayed for like thirty minutes. He told me, "You are a powerful man of God." I said thank you. He said, "You are welcome, no problem."

I told him, "May the Lord bless you and have a blessed day." He said thank you. Then, I said, "You are welcome." After that, I continued to walk around the park. While I was walking around the park, I saw something on this bench by the water fountain. I kept walking, ignoring what it was.

I walked by the second time. I stopped and looked to see what it was. I went over to the bench by the water fountain. I looked to see what it was. It was a loaf of bread, just sitting there. It was some Butter Split Top Wheat Bread. I grabbed it and looked at it. There was nothing wrong with the bread.

It had not even been opened. The bread was not touched. I put it down and left it where it was, and started back walking around the park. I stopped and went back to the bench by the water fountain where the bread was. I grabbed the bread again and went home with it.

When I got home with the loaf of bread, I made some toast with some honey and ate it up. When I ate, I had drool all around my mouth. Then, when I got through with it, I went to my room and prayed, "Thank you, Lord, for the bread I have received."

When I got through with that, I went back to the kitchen. I got a can of green beans, some salad, and some fish. I made a thing of green beans and a salad. Then, I made two pieces of fish. I made some more toast, put it all on a plate, and fixed it up. I had made a meal out of the bread.

I prayed over my meal. I said, "Lord, thank you for this food I received. Thank you for the loaf of bread I have received. Please make this food I received make me full." I ate that food and it was great. After I finished, I got up and went to the park. While I was walking, my belly was full of food. I was happy that I had gotten something to eat.

It was on a Saturday when that happened. I went to the park, prayed, and found a big loaf of bread. It was a good day. I always remember the time that I prayed and got the loaf of bread at the park. Praying is a good thing. If I could make a program, I would call it Pray Together. It would be a Christian program. Praying together is a gift from God. It is the Holy Spirit guiding you and directing you, and leading you in the ways in life! If you pray in tongue, that is the Holy Spirit guiding you! Just praying together is a beautiful thing.

You just have to love that blessing. That is a gift, just like giving. Giving is a blessing and you just have to get it. The Wondrous Works of God are a blessing in our lives. Use the gifts that God gave us. That is how we get more blessings in our lives. As we come and go, just get the blessings that you need.

The manifestation from the Lord is to have that door of blessings open for you. You have the open door of blessings to walk in to! We all need blessings in our lives. We just have to keep the blessings we get from Jesus. Keep God first most of all. We have to be strong in our lives. Just praying everyday will bless our lives. Just hope that everything will come together.

I pray for the Lord to bless himself all the time while He is doing His Wondrous Works! Heaven is His throne and earth is His foot stool. Being here on earth, we have to praise and worship Him. Give Him your all because He is our one and only Father. The word of God is what we need to hear every day.

We need to hear His word. We have to study every day in our lives. We all have the time to do it. As I keep moving, I think about His word. It gives me the strength to keep on moving and stay strong as I am in these days of struggle! We all face challenges and go through things every day in our lives. We have to put up with things every day in our lives.

We have to try to overcome our enemies every day! It is important to try to overcome everything we face and everything that happens. We have to do better than the people we do not want to see or hear. As I pray, my enemies are in the Lord's hands. They say always pray for your enemy. That was what I was doing at the time. I would pray every day and every night that I got the strength to move on.

I am always hoping for a great life. Life is beautiful and I expect to enjoy every minute of it! The prayers of the Lord's people are within me, telling me that the power and strength are within me!

I will overcome any challenge that I face in life by getting my strength in life from the King of Kings and the Lord of Lords! I can do all things through Jesus Christ who strengthens me. Having the Wondrous Works of God in my life is a blessing and brings joy to my life! It is the Wondrous Works of God in my life that make me joyful.

I love having the mercy of the Lord in my life, the mercy I wake up with every morning, and the mercy that lets me still have my family in my life! Mercy, mercy, mercy me! By the grace of God, I will overcome my enemies. By the grace of God, I will make it in these days. I will keep moving strong and holding on to life. By His mercy and grace, I will have many successes.

I will overcome challenges that I am facing. It will be by the mercy and grace of God that I will do this. I know that the days get better! The sky does get clearer. The sky will get bluer. The days will get better. I have hope that everything will come together! All things will come together in Jesus' name.

We should keep giving the Lord all the glory for what He has done for us. We should praise and worship Him every day in our lives. Pray that our problems go away, so we can have the freedom to do what we want to do. It is a blessing to have our freedom!

It feels good when you have your freedom to get out and relax when you want, and to get up in the morning with peace! Just to be alone sometimes is a good thing. Having your own freedom is good. Just taking a deep breath and saying that I am free at last feels good, just as it was for blacks during slavery!

Freedom is the best thing to have. For all our problems in life, freedom is a good thing. In our lifetime, we must come together if we want to pick up the broken pieces and shattered dreams that we had. This country we are in is about to fall apart. Today, we must do what needs to be done out here in this world.

Being departed from the world, we will not struggle to do what needs to be done. If we come together with Jesus Christ, we will overcome the days that we are fighting. Our mind is where the battle is. Every day is a battle we have to fight. Keep fighting the battle as you are entering the battlefield!

If you are not prepared as you are entering the battlefield, it is like going to war without a weapon. You always have to be prepared for what to do. Life is not a joke and you have to fight battles out here in the world. I just hope that I will see the days get better in my sight. Pray for this country and that God will bless America!

Bless this country at the time that things need to change. The change is coming and we have to be ready for the greater days that are coming. I pray that the Lord will heal the world we are in. Lord, bless the children during all of this violence. We have so much violence and killing of innocent children and people in this country.

While I am still living in this world, I'll keep taking a breath and taking a step! Walking in the spirit of the Lord, I will continue to be strong out here in my life! I will spend my lifetime taking a step forward trying to see the days getting better. In the times of struggle, people want the days to get better and that's what we are fighting for.

I'm just hoping things will get better than what we are seeing with our eyes. Time is flying by and some things are not changing. We have to work together to make the changes happen. Working together will make things much easier for this world we are living in today. Pray that we will see the changes!

Just pray to God and thank Him for the blessings we have now. The change will come; you just have to hold on. Hold on with all of your power and strength! Stand up for what is right. We have to do the right things in our lives to keep us going. Those changes are happening in our lives.

We see the sunshine in our eyes in the morning when we wake up. Thank God for waking us up in the morning. When I was living in Dallas, I would always trust in God for everything I did. I pray and hope that I will get stronger as I walk in these days. I'm just holding on to the power and strength in my lifetime! I will continue holding on, being strong, staying strong, going strong, and moving strong.

In these times, I just pray to carry on! As I continue to pray, I get stronger and keep moving on. I get more wisdom and knowledge as I carry on. In our lifetime, guidance from the Holy Spirit is what we need. We need Jesus Christ in our lives. We need help from the Lord.

The only way we can get it is by praying. Ask the Holy Spirit to show us which way to go! Praying together will give us more faith in what we are doing. Have the faith to know we can overcome our challenges. Know that we are more than conquerors. Know that we have the victory! We have the victory, my brothers and sisters, over this foolishness that we are in today.

All of this foolishness that is going on in this country is silly! There is too much foolishness going on today. There is too much going on. Like I said, it is sometimes like there is nobody out there trying to end it. We are walking in these days with so much going on! People are out here just praying for the world. I really do not care for this world.

I hear all these great things about the world! Then, I hear the bad about the world! I care about entering heaven, rather than being on earth. Heaven is His throne. Earth is His foot stool. It is easy for Him to come to us and do what He wants to do. The power of God is strong. The power of the Almighty God is strong. It is so strong that man will fear Him forever.

The Almighty God is doing the Wondrous Works of God in our lives. He is the eternal spirit of life doing His spiritual works. The Holy Spirit is in our lives! The Father, Son, the Holy Ghost, the Holy Trinity, and Almighty God himself! Sometimes, when I was younger, I would just pray for the Holy Trinity. Back then when I was younger, I would call it Holy Matrimony.

I used to do that when I was younger. I would feel good about myself every day when I would get out. I was just as joyful as I could be in my life when I was younger; having the blessing that God is on my side and knowing that I was going to win all my battles!

I knew that I would have the victory in my life! I knew that I would have the victory! Know that you have the victory! Back then when I was ten years old, having God in my life was important. Jesus Christ is my best friend and my one and only father. He loves me so much that He came to see me in my life.

Give God all we can give Him in our lifetime. It does not take much for us to show our love. He can give everything to us to show how much He loves us. There is not enough that we can give. In the days of our lifetime, we are praising and worshipping Him. Most people blame God for what has happened in their lives. I cannot blame Him for anything.

I always blame myself. I have never thought of blaming anything on Jesus Christ. If you are blaming anything on God, you are in the flesh. Just pray for yourself that you will have better days in your life. Things will come together if you just keep putting God first. Always put God first in your life.

Things will come together in Jesus' name. As they say, just keep the faith. They say by faith we understand. That is one thing people say. It is the truth, by faith we understand. We do not live by sight and the mind. We live by spirit and faith.

We live life by the faith we have. Just pray to Him to give us a whole lot of faith in our life! Be strong! Have the courage to do the things you need to do. Have the strength to move on! We have to carry on our lives in the right way!

Have high self-esteem and keep on moving! I was building up my strength to get ready to get on a new path way. I was getting ready to get on the new path way, trying to get to a new journey in life! I pray that the days will get better!

I'm being strong in my life so I can carry on. I have to carry on! I will carry on with a whole lot of faith as I am moving strong in the days. I'm moving strong in the days with my power and strength! I will carry on by having faith that I will move on to better days.

I carry myself in a good way so nobody wants to think badly about me. I will continue to keep doing that and build myself up where nobody will put me down. I'm carrying on at the time so that I will continue to move strong! I will carry on as I am moving strong and walking in the spirit.

As we walk in the spirit, let us live in the spirit. I'm walking in the spirit of the Lord in my lifetime! I'll just praise the Lord as I am walking in the spirit! As I am praying every day, I am moving strong. I'll continue to pray with people I do not know, just to see things come together! I pray that I will walk in the open doors of blessings!

I pray that the blessings will come into my life! I know that the good times are going to come into my life! Let the Holy Spirit lead me and guide me in my life. Let the Holy Spirit lead me and direct me in my life. I have the Wondrous Works of God in my life! I love thinking about what God has done for me.

I just have to give Him my all for what He has done in my life. I will continue to move strong in the days!

CHAPTER 9

THE END OF THE DAYS AND TIME

As I remember the days and the time when things happened, I continue to stay strong walking in the spirit of the Lord. I remembered the time when they had drug lords where I lived. I was moving back and forth trying to be happy while things were going on. While I was moving on, I was still praying with people I did not know.

I try to stay strong as I am moving forward and walking in the spirit of the Lord! I saw all of these things going on! All the things that were going on, for some reason, looked like they would not come to an end. All of this foolishness that is going on around this country is not stopping! Some people are just praying for this world.

Just pray for what is going on around this world of today. Seeing all of the stuff that is going on around this country is sad! All of these tragedies are happening and some people are not trying to solve them. We have all of this violence going on! I'm just trying to have faith, hope, peace, and love in my life. I'm just carrying on in my lifetime as I am witnessing what is going on.

"What's Going On?" What's going on out here in these days of tragedy? I am a witness to other people in the struggle for the Lord Jesus Christ! In my lifetime, I'm walking in the spirit of the Lord, trying to make it. Pray together to stay strong and survive in the times. I am living my life at this time and trying to make it. In these days of tragedy, why are we not working together? We might continue to struggle because we do not have partnership.

Working together will make things a whole lot better than what it is now. My teachers have been telling me things will get better if we just work together. One said, "You have all these people working by themselves and not working together. It would be a whole lot better if we could just work together."

Working together would make this country better than what it is. From what I have been hearing, this country is falling apart. This country is on the down fall because of all that is going on. He has been telling me all of these things and I am just going to say they are true. I hear all these things that are going on and I hear what he is saying.

I was just surprised about what I was hearing about all the things that were going on in the United States of America! In the United States of America, all these tragedies are going on. Too much violence is going on in the United States of America! There is too much killing involved in this country.

You have people that say how great this country is. Then, you have people saying how bad this country is. I just do not know what to say about this country we are in. The only times I can remember are the good times. I have to build up myself as I carry on in these times! I have to have high self-esteem to carry myself in a good way.

I am holding on to the power and strength of my lifetime! I am here in the days of the tragedies that are going on! When I think about the times when things were going on, the only thing I can do is just pray for me. The only thing I can do is pray.

I have all this anger from what is going on. Living this life, I see all these things going on. I just have to keep praying and carrying myself on in these days. Seeing the things that are going on out here in these places, I just have to have the power and strength to carry on. I see myself going by in all of these tragedies that are going on.

That's what people talked about every day. I was praying and hoping that the days would get better for me at that time. I prayed to have the strength to move day by day in those places! I sometimes wished that I would get out of that place! It was hard seeing all of that stuff going on every day.

I had to pray with people I did not know, just to give me strength to carry on in life. I was building up my faith, knowing that I would make it out there and hoping that I would continue to be blessed to wake up joyful every day!

I woke up every morning to catch the train to make it to the training academy. I was blessed that I was not getting put down from anything else. Waking up in the morning, I saw the struggles of young men and women out there! The young men lounging their pants had low self-esteem, and did not believe that they could do well in life.

Most of the time, they were putting down themselves. They were using bad language to communicate. As Christian people, we call ourselves brothers and sisters, and we have to pray for and believe in one another. These days, people are waiting for Jesus to come. Pray every day of your life that we receive blessings in our lives! Try to keep walking in to the open door of blessings!

We want the manifestation of the Lord! We need that door to open so we can get the blessings! The manifestation is what some people need. I am walking in the spirit of the Lord, so I can make it every day! Time is going by as the days are flying by! Just pray that things will come together.

I remember when that seven year old got shot up in the school. I do not see how someone could do a terrible thing like that. It is like they are working for Satan in their life. Who could do such a thing like killing innocent children? They must be all wound up with negative thoughts in their mind. Everything they say and do must be negative.

You are really sold out to the devil if you are doing things like that. Satan is the Father of lies and you must not hear him. Keep giving God all the glory and He will make a way for you. No one loves at all a person killing innocent children. You are a criminal for killing innocent children! God is going to send you to hell. He will not forgive you your sins for what you have done if you are living a life full of crime!

As I move strong in the days, I will remember this. As I am strongly walking in the spirit of the Lord, I pray that I see better days. I'm living this life, seeing all of this foolishness that is going on. I have to wonder how this stuff is happening.

These people do not have any help out here. They are just trying to make it in these times of struggle! As some people say, the days of crisis are here. We are struggling in this country to make things right! I have to walk in the spirit of the Lord in my lifetime. The only thing I can do is pray and that is what I have to keep doing.

I just want to walk in the open doors of blessings, just so I can be joyful when I wake up in the morning. We are in the times that all the struggles are happening. Time to get it together in this country! Time to put the tragedies to an end! Just pray that things will come together!

We are going through the days with the Lord on our side! Hold on to the power and strength of a lifetime! Being in the days of tragedy, I am trying to make it in this life. I wish that everything would come together! I can see myself in the days of the tragedy holding on.

I am trying to make it out here in this world! I pray every day that things will get better! I remember the times that I was getting out and seeing all the women! I was enjoying myself as I was out at midnight! I was seeing the moonlight at night, talking, and letting the good times roll. Letting the good times roll!

Being out there with all those beautiful women, I could not help just to get out there every night. I wished we could party all the time, like every day was a holiday in our lives. We could not party all our lives because we had to work, so we could make it in our lives. We saw all those things that were going on! We were building ourselves up so we could be ready for our days ahead!

Thank God for waking us up every morning to see the sunshine in our lives that is putting a smile on our faces! We want the good life every day in our life! We need to spend time with our loved ones, saying that we love each other! We should have good times with our family and friends.

I remember the time that I graduated from school. I enjoyed having everybody give me a gift card for graduation! I did not even know how good it was to graduate from school. I thought it was nothing at the time. Everyone was just proud of me. I thought it was really nothing.

Then, I graduated from a mechanic school. It took a two hour train ride to get back home! I saw all of these things happening on the way back! I looked at problems come and go. I saw all of these things going on in this country. In those days, we are reading the newspaper. We read about all these things that were going on. Hope and pray that the days will get better!

We see all of the things that are going on around these places! All of this violence is going on! Too much of it is causing problems that some people cannot solve. I want all of these bad things to end out here in these deep places where all these things are going on.

There is all of this hating and jealousy going on! On the train, I'm going by looking at what is going on around those areas. I live this life seeing all of this going on! I see violence fighting, hating, and everything else going on! I just want to get away from these things that are going on! I'm still going on as the days are flying by! Pray and hope that things will come together.

I was going to church every day to praise and worship the Lord. I remembered the times that I was seeing things! I remembered how I did not pray for those people that needed to be prayed for. After what they had been doing, I was not going to help them. I thought that I did not need to pray for them and that I just needed to pray for myself. What was going on at that time?

I need to make it out here in this time of struggle. The days of tragedy are something else. We have all these problems that need to be fixed! We want everything to come together! We woke up in the morning and wished that everything would be better at the time! Thank him for the blessings that we have for right now. Just be positive about what is going on at this time.

I was lifting myself up in those positive times, hoping things would go right. I was making myself get it together so that I would be alright at that time! I wanted to see the happy days in my life! All of it would come together pretty soon. The broken pieces and shattered dreams would be fixed. I saw all these people struggling at the time! We need to pray and love one another so we can make it a better place. At the places I would go by, they were not doing much, but I just hoped it would get better.

I wanted things to get better as the days were going by. I saw all of these things that were going on around that place. In the deep areas, there were a whole lot of things going on! I had to witness all of those things that were going on at that time! None of this was good. I wanted all the things to come together!

I was seeing drug addicts and fighting. All of these things were no good. I wanted all of it to come to an end! I prayed that the days would get better and better. We need to keep walking in the spirit of the Lord in our lifetime! I knew that I would be alright as long as I was with God, getting led and directed by the Holy Spirit. I pray that I will continue to depend on the Lord!

I remember the days that I was just hearing the sweet old music! I was hearing the sweet old music and getting out the house as I was moving on. I was out there having fun and enjoying life at the time. I saw the moonlight at nighttime when I was out there with a lot of people! There was loud music and people talking and enjoying themselves! I was having all this fun!

There was so much stuff going on around those places! It just looked like no one was really trying to help those people. The young men and women needed help out there with all of these things they were going through. All of those young men and young women were struggling!

One time, I prayed for those people. I prayed that all of their problems would be solved! You just have to keep praying for them. It was not easy out there in the world where we were. Out there in those places, people needed help, but there was no one trying to help them. I'll keep praying for the people that need help in their lives, hoping that everything will be alright for them!

At this time, the days of tragedy will continue on if there is nobody willing to help this country. We have a world full of chaos at this time! I remember when I used to walk in the rain trying to get a job! I did not have to, but I used to do it. I was out there trying to get on my feet, hoping that I would see the better days out here in the days of tragedy!

I was always wishing that things would come together at the time! I was trying to pull myself together with my power and strength all the time, just trying to make it out here. I was in the days of the struggle, trying to get things together and waiting for the change to come! I held on like a soldier to stay strong at the time.

Pray to be full of the Word of God in the spirit. Take about one day being in nothing but the spirit! One guy says if Jesus took us from our bodies to be in the spirit, we would be walking through the walls. Sometimes, we have our talk about being in the spirit, praising and worshipping, and giving God all the glory.

I see all of these days flying by. I would go to church every Sunday to give God all the glory! I remember the times of going to church praising and worshipping the Lord! I remember doing that dance in church that I had people talking about! I also remember the times that I thought God wanted me to do something.

Being in Bible study, I had my own thing going on. People there enjoyed me at the time, calling me a witness of God for seeing all of this violence, hatred, and jealousy that was going on! I was a witness of all those things that were going on out there in those deep places! So much was going on in those times!

Sometimes life is war and everyday is a battle you have to fight. Get prepared for the wars and battles we have to fight. Be in the battlefield like a soldier with a machine gun. Get ready to let out all the chaos that has been going on! I'm ready to overcome my enemy that is out there in the battlefield! We see so many enemies wanting to take us on in the battlefield!

We go to war and fight the battles that are going on every day. We want the best out of life for ourselves! Pray that the days will get better! Let's fill ourselves with hope that we will make it! Pay attention to all of this foolishness that is going on around here in these places!

I remember when I worked in a meat market with the guys. I remember when we talked and had fun and enjoyed ourselves while we were working. I'm just remembering the times I had there and the times when I was not there. I did not trust anybody! I thought no one cared for me. I just remember all those times that I had been doing some work!

Looking forward to the days ahead, I hope that the good times will come in. I try to stay focused on doing what I need to do. I'm trying to keep my head straight so I can stay moving in the right direction and keep going on the right path. I see so many days going by! I just pray that I will see the days that everything will come together!

I'm keeping my eyes on the Lord, hoping that I will rejoice! I'm trying to fight the enemy and trying not to cry at the time! I remember when I used to drink a beer when I felt like crying. I would go outside just singing the sweet old music in those days! I was looking at the time fly by and watching the days go by faster and faster. Every morning, I would pray, "Thank you, God, for waking me up this morning!"

I wished that all of my dreams would come true one day! I would walk around the park at the water fountain and throw up coins into the water like a wishing well, wishing one day that I would be rich! I would pray near the water fountain that I would be blessed during the time, wishing that I could see Jesus again! He had seen me once. I just wish He would see me again.

He is with me everywhere I go. I just wish to see Him in person. You are blessed if you see God. I just want to be blessed in my life because I have Jesus as my one and only father! I was just walking around the park, hoping that everything would come together.

Going to the park and praying together, God's children were coming together to give God the glory in His Holy name! It was a blessing every day to wake up in the morning and see the sunshine in my eyes. I love being a servant for the Lord and having my light shine in other people lives! Some of those people, I do not even know! I just love being a blessing to other people!

Pray for one another when times are going wrong! Be strong and stay strong when things are not going right. Pray that it will be peaceful during the storms we are going through. We want blessings in our lives so that we will be alright. Hope that things will go right! Wish that all of our problems will go away and we will feel better about ourselves.

Feel better when things are working out right. Hope that we will feel better and that everything goes the way we want it to go. If everything goes our way, we would be a whole lot better than what we are today. Most of us would not be complaining where we are today. Pray that we get the manifestation of the Lord!

Pray that the door would open and we walk in to get the blessings. Walk in the open door of blessings, where all the blessings are and we can get them. The blessings come from the Holy land! The Kingdom of God waits for us to come in. We have a whole lot of studying to do.

I would pray at the park to do all the things according to the Word of God! I hope that our lives will get better than what it is. I wish to see better days in our lives! I hope nothing will hurt us. There is nothing like the times when we have fallen flat on our faces! Not even the times when we get depressed. There is nothing like those times in our lives! We do not want anything to harm us. We want the better times in our lives to come in!

As we are praying together, we are praying that everything will be better. Then Jesus should really have his own way! Besides hearing from man in our lives, pray together that we will make it in our lives. Pray that we will be fine as we are walking and talking in the spirit. Pray that as we are living in the spirit, we will be fine as we are going through the storm!

Pray that we get out of the storm! We want to see the sun shining in our lives, and we want to put a great big smile on our faces. Live in the spirit, knowing that we will be alright! Pray that we will be in nothing but the spirit in our lives! Pray that we will not be in the flesh and in the spirit! When the good days come, we will be in nothing but the spirit.

I see the days going on as the time is flying by. The time is flying by as we are in the spirit! I see the Lord Jesus Christ in our lives! Pray that we will see Him face to face one day! Know everything will come together at the right time.

I see the days getting better as we are praying together! Pray that we will be strong in our lives! Pray that we will have the strength and power to move on in the days going forward! Always try to take a step forward in this life we are in. I still see all of this tragedy that we are going through! I still see the hating, violence, and jealousy that are going around.

Let's pray for ourselves so that we get a blessing in our lives! We want everything to be fair, but life is not fair. We just want that blessing in life. We want to walk in that open door of blessings in our lives. See the Wondrous Works of God in our lives! Know that He is worthy of everything that He does!

He is the Great I Am. He is the only perfect one and we just have to keep praising Him. They say our good is as filthy as a dirty rag and we have a whole lot of work to do, being in this world that Almighty God loves. For God so loved the world, He sent His only begotten Son. People say things about the world, but I do not know. God loves the world so much that He sent us Jesus.

If it would not have been for Jesus, we would still be in our evil ways. We would still be doing the wrong things. Jesus turned everyone's life around, and gave us eternal life. One day we will drink the living water in our lives. That is when we will see Him and be with Him for all eternity. We want the blessings that we love to get in our lives today! We want so much more in our lives! Pray that the days will get better!

There are so many of us praying people who have a lot of power. The power of praying people! We live in the spirit in our life, knowing that we will be alright! Praying together has given me more strength during my lifetime. The Holy Spirit has shown me which way to go in life. I pray that God keeps doing his Wondrous Works of God in our lives!

I see the better days coming by and am hoping that we will get better by praising every day! I know that God loves us in our lives. God wants the best for us and we have to accept what He is doing. Even the little blessings in our lives matter! Better is little with the fear of the Lord, than great treasure and the trouble therewith!

Just accept the little blessings and hope that everything will go right in our lives. We are blessed to have Jesus Christ as our Lord and Savior! Know that He loves us with all His heart! Know that He loves us before we love Him! Know that He is the Father of the truth!

He is the Bread of Life! The bread that we need every day! He knew us before He sent us to earth. He knew us way before we opened our eyes. He had planned out what was going to happen in our lives. We just have to make the right decisions and choices in our lives and go on the right path!

Seek God and obey Him for what He wants us to do. We are blessed to see the sunshine in our eyes! Know that God is going to bless us in our life! Hoping that everything will come together at the time! We have the blessing of praying together! We get to see God working things out in our lives! Have faith, hope, peace, and love for our Lord Jesus Christ. We have the blessings that we need in our lives!

I remember all the times that have gone by. I hope that God will change everything that I am seeing out there! We are still praying together as the time is flying by. I know that blessings are going to come my way! I will be caught up in a whirlwind with the Word by having God in my life!

Better days are coming; I just have to hold on and wait for the good times to rock in! I am happy with where I am right now. I wonder if I will see the days that will get better! I know that God has something in store for me! I am just getting ready for the blessings to come in as I am praying together with people that I don't know!

I think of the country and what we are going through. As I am thinking of everything else to pray about, I do not even pray for the country. We usually pray for ourselves, besides the country. We usually lift each other's spirits, instead of praying for this country. We pray for ourselves and what God has done for us.

We pray for the blessings we need, instead of for the country. We do everything else, except pray for the country. We need to help ourselves instead of taking care of someone else. My teacher always told me to take care of myself. I always remembered what she said. I had always put myself before anybody else till I started to trust in people!

I started to pray for other people, instead of just for myself. I learned to love others as I was in the spirit! We were just praying and loving one another, as the Bible says. I kept being a good child of God in my life!

I remembered the time I worked in the meat market. I really enjoyed those times when I worked in the meat market. I had fun with the guys I worked with. I was trying to be strong at the time as I was going on. I could see happy days at that time in my life! I was working and going to school at the same time. I was just out there in Dallas trying to make it in that time. I was in the spirit out there trying to make it. I was still seeing all of these things going on as I was out there going to school!

Most of this was probably coming from where they were from. The young ones need help and there was no one there to help them. I did not have to worry back then because if someone was trying to mistreat you, God would always handle the problem. I prayed that times would get better at the time!

I was hoping that God would bless the people that were lost out there in those places! I know that Jesus is the way for people to get help! Jesus would save them from those times, as He loves everyone that is here on earth! He will bless those with needs in their life. He will comfort you with His spirit. He will be there for you when you need Him. He will make things work out for all of your problems you have.

He will shine His light in your life and put a smile on your face. Everything He does is wonderful. You just have to thank Him for how good of a God He is. He loves you with all of His heart. He wants the best for you in your life. He loves us!

I remembered the time that I found that loaf of bread at the park! I was just recalling those times and how I thanked God for what I found. Then, I was able to make a meal out of the bread that I found! I thanked the Lord for the food I received. I give Him all the glory for what He has done for me. He is the one and only father in my life. I accept the blessings that He has given me in my life!

I'm still watching the days going on as the time is flying by. I see the Works of God that are in my life! I am happy that He is in my life! I hoped for so much good to happen at the time. I accept the blessings that I am getting right now and am letting Him show me which way to go in my life! I pray that so much will happen at the time.

I am blessed to wake up to see the sunshine in the morning! I thank God for showing me which way to go in life. It has to be a blessing that He is with me with every step I take. I am making the right decisions in life! I'm letting God work inside me and make me a new creature!

I pray to do everything according to the Word of God! I pray to be fulfilled with the Word of God in my spirit. I want the best out of my life! Seeing the types of days that I am seeing now, I did not expect things like this to happen to me. Then, I see all of the things that are going on.

I did not think stuff like this was happening. All of these tragedies are going on in people's lives. I am holding on with all of my power and strength in my lifetime, knowing that God has something in store for me in my life! I'm going in the right ways in my lifetime, making sure I do not make the wrong decisions in my life. His word is a lamp for my feet and a light for my path. His commandment is a lamp. His law is a light. There are the reproofs of instructions that guide the ways of life. I am walking in the spirit of the Lord, praying that I will be alright! I see the sunshine in my eyes and the better days ahead of me!

I want the good times to come in! I am staying strong as I am out here in these places at the time! I will keep going strong as I am moving forward in my life! I will continue to hold on as I am trying to make it in this day. I want to get out of this foolishness that is going on!

What's up! What happening around here, my brothers and sisters? I see so many struggling out here in these places! It is time to get it together for these people out here. I want them to have good days in their lives! I pray that they will be happy in their lives! I wish that they would have better days in their lives. I feel sad for what they are going through in their lives.

I want the best for these people in the struggle! I pray that God will lift them up in the spirit and wish that all of their problems would go away. I rebuke Satan in the name of Jesus! I want them to conquer every problem they have in their life. We are more than conquerors and we can beat every challenge we face.

As we are going through all of these challenges, I pray that we will overcome all of them at the time! I know that God has something planned for us at the time! We will continue to pull and lift ourselves up in our lives. I want us to come out strong in the battle that we are fighting! Keep lifting Jesus up to make it through what we are going through.

We go through trials and tribulations in our lives. I see the happy days coming forward in our lives! Trying to stay spiritual lifted in these times is hard. Challenges are coming in our lives. The only thing I can do is just pray about it and continue walking in the spirit of the Lord! I am staying strong as I am moving on in time! I am moving strong as I am in the days. I am walking, talking, guiding, and directing in the spirit of the Lord!

Lifting myself up, I am moving on in time! I'm going strong everywhere I go out here. I am trying to stay strong as I am moving on in these times! I am taking a deep breath and getting out in these deep areas. I'm praying for myself and for people that I know from where I am from.

I hope for the best for everyone! I pray that I will get blessed going out here in these areas. I see all the struggles that people are talking about! I did not know all of this was going on. It is like God is showing me everything that is going on. That is why people were calling me a witness at the time. I am seeing all of the foolishness that is going on occurring at the time. I know that one day it will all come to an end.

CHAPTER 10

THE END OF THE DAYS OF TRAGEDY

I'm still moving strong, going back and forth, in these times! I know that so much is not going to happen. As I walk on through these places, I see the tragedies occurring. I stay strong while walking up and down the street! I know one day all of this will come to an end. The days of tragedy are going by every day.

Seeing all of this going on, the only thing I can do is pray. I say my prayers every day in my life. That is the only thing I can do. I just want them to get an understanding of what is really going on out here in these places. I see all of these young people struggling out here, lounging their pants and trying to fight one another.

There is so much hating and jealousy for one another! It's just not helping the situation. It is just making things worse in life. All of this fighting and jealousy are just making things worse. It is getting no better out there any other place. Times are just getting worse and worse by the minute.

It's hard being in a position where you can hardly do anything for yourself. Hopefully, one day you will get out of this foolishness going on where you are from. It's like being stuck in a real life movie and you cannot get out. Being in these times is hard every day! Keep trying to make it out here in these types of places where hardly anything great is going on.

Always keep your head straight and just keep pressing forward at the time. I am living in the spirit in my lifetime! I am staying in the spirit in my lifetime! I am walking in the spirit trying to make it out here in these places! We have to be angry about what is going on out here at the time. You see so much that you wish you could end.

You want the best for people out here because you are tired of seeing them struggle! Know that Jesus will work things out! Be blessed in knowing that he will make a way for you! We see all of these times of struggle where all of these people are killing each other. Black people are even killing blacks, hating their own people!

We do not want to pray with each other or help one another at the time. You have all these struggles within yourself and you wish things would come together for yourself. Be strong in these days! I know that I will carry myself in a right way! I am keeping my head straight so I can continue to keep taking a step forward in the time!

As I say, in the mean time, keep on striking. Just keep on taking a step forward. Take it one day at a time! As I am moving in and out in this lifetime, I am holding on with the power and strength. I pray that I will carry on during this time! I pray that I will be a blessing as I am going out in these days!

I know that God is on my side! I hope everything will come together at the time. I will stay strong so I can continue to move forward as I am in the days-the days of tragedy! These are the days of crisis. These are the days of struggle! We are in the days of hard times. We have to pray together to stay strong in these times of tragedy!

I am still going all out in the days of tragedy! I feel like I am in the inside as an insider having the inner city blues playing! It makes me want to move out of this country and move to a different area. I have to be strong to make it out here in these areas! I know that something bad is going to happen every day in this time!

I keep pulling myself up to be strong as I am in the days! I am trying to be as strong as I was back then. I remember the time when I was working out in the back yard-not staying strong by drinking a strong beer-I mean staying strong by lifting weights. I was using all of my power and strength to make it out here in those days-the days of tragedy- that were going on.

Walk forward and go straight ahead for what you need. Do what you are supposed to do. Just keep on moving in these times. Pray that we will survive out here in the days of tragedy! I'm going in and out of the places where people need help. Lord Jesus, help these people in the days of tragedy. Bless them that they will be protected out here! These places do not have any love and all this needs to come to an end. It's time to put an end to all of the foolishness that is going on out here. We only have a few heroes that will end all of this that is going on. Continue to move strong in these times. Try to live the life that you want out here!

So much is going on at these times of the day. You just have to keep moving strong. Like I said, hold on with the power and strength of your lifetime! You continually have to move forward and keep taking it step by step. Take it one day at a time! I'm getting myself together to keep moving forward in these days of tragedy!

I want to see that blessing come around at the time! I am expecting a blessing to come around my way in life! I just want to be a blessing in life! I will keep my head straight as I am moving strong in the days. I will hold on till I make it out here in this time of the day.

I will try to keep moving straight ahead! I will just continue to keep my trust in God. I will just keep trusting God so that I will make it in due time. I know that He has something planned for me in my life! I pray that I will have the strength to move on in the days! I am walking in the spirit so I can just keep going on the right path way.

I will keep living in the spirit so I can be blessed to see a blessed day. Praising and worshipping Jesus Christ, I'll thank Him for what He has done for me in life. I know that there is only one true God in our lives! I have to thank Him for waking me up every morning to be blessed to see the next day ahead! I want to be a blessing in my life!

I am just continually moving forward in this lifetime! I will just have to keep my head straight. I want to stay on the right path way in life, so I will continue doing good. I want to continue doing well so God will be proud of me! He is going to love me anyway, whether I am doing bad or good at the time.

Pray together to lift up our spirit in need! We want to get a blessing out of our lives! Know that God loves us with all His heart! He wants the best to come out of our lives! Pray together that we will continue to keep moving on the right path way in life! Stay strong as we continue to move in time! I will move strong as I am in the days.

I am trying to make it out here in this place! In the battlefield, we are fighting the battle to make it! We are fighting wars that are going on in these areas! Living in the spirit, I will get blessed in time. I am holding on to the Lord's hands just so I can make it. I see better days ahead that will put a smile on my face.

Going forward, I will continue to move strong in all types of situations that I am going through. I will take a step forward so I can get a blessing out of life! I will continue on going as I am walking in the spirit! Being fulfilled in the spirit with faith, I have to try to stay strong!

I am staying strong for what might happen out here at the time. Only God knows what can happen. I just have to be strong because there is no telling what can happen. No telling what will happen in a day's time.

I see myself moving forward in these days of tragedy! I will continue to move on to get where I need to be. I will stay strong to move on in this lifetime! I want the best out of life! I pray that I will get blessed as I am moving forward in time. I am trying to stay strong in this time of struggle in this country! This is the time when we need a change!

Walking in the spirit, I pray every day that I will make it! In the hard times in my life, I know that God has something planned for me in my life! I wish that everything would come to hand during all of these times! I want to be proud of when I have success. I plan to make it in the future!

Go in the right way unto the Lord! Let the Lord have his way in our lives. Be blessed to see a new day in our lives! I am living in the spirit as I am moving on in the days! I'm getting tired of hearing and seeing what is going on out here in these areas. All of this foolishness that is going on needs to stop!

The foolishness needs to be put to an end! All of this chaos is going on at the time. Pray to the Lord, "Let there be peace during the storm." In the battlefield, try to overcome the enemy! Fight with our power and strength while trying to win the battle!

I am trying to conquer all of the problems that I have! I see the great place near the battlefield! A place to rest and relax! I am waiting till everything ends in this war that I am in. I am taking my place where the battle will start, moving in where all the chaos is happening. I will be strong so I can make it in the time!

I am holding on with my last deep breath, taking advantage while I have the chance to win! I am being strong as I am in the days of the war, fighting with all ammunition to have this war put to an end. I will use the biggest weapon I can use. I will continue to hold on to God's hand, wishing that I could live on to see the better days.

Franklon Rashuaude Voss is a young African American man from a predominantly African American part of Plano, Texas. He is a young man trying to do what God commanded of him-write books. He is working hard to turn his dream into a reality. He came from Downtown Plano, and has seen and experienced a lot of violence in the past.

For more information, write to FranklonRashaudeVoss@yahoo.com.

ABOUT THE AUTHOR

The author that wrote this book is a young African American man named Franklon Rashaude Voss. Voss is a Christian that people are calling a witness of God and a True Prophet from the Lord. He was born in Plano, Texas. He came from an area known as Downtown Plano. It was a ghetto that had a lot of violence in the neighborhoods. There are still things happening in that neighborhood today. Voss is an African-American that has been through a whole lot of struggle.

Voss has gone from struggling in an African American part of a city, to being a boy that went through depression that could have taken his life, to experiencing times where people in the family were not doing right, to being a black boy that had problems seeing Satan, until Jesus Christ came to see him. If you want to know more about how Jesus Christ came to see him, read the book of John in the Living Translation Holy Bible.

He was an African American boy that had the dreams of being an NBA player. He was on the middle and high school basketball teams. He played 7th, 8th, and 9th grade basketball. He was a school basketball All-Star until his dreams came crashing down due to one of his struggles.

He had problems seeing Satan and lost his mind at the young age of 13 years old. He quit playing because he was not as strong as he used to be, and he had problems with his grades in 9th grade when he played basketball. The struggle was so bad that he lost his mind and the school put him in classes for the mentally challenged. They found out he was not mentally challenged when he made the 9th grade basketball team for his third time in a row. He was a good player and people knew him everywhere. Everyone thought his dreams were easily going to come true.

Unfortunately, that did not happen. When he was 13 years old, Voss had problems seeing Satan, the fallen angel that Almighty God kicked out of heaven! Franklon Rashaude Voss could have been dead, but Jesus Christ came to see him in person to save him from Satan. People never thought that Voss would have had his dreams crash down around him, but as they say, it happens to the best of us. Voss has grown up to be a man that depends on the Lord Jesus Christ.

Voss has given testimonies in church about what he has been through. He has turned his life around and he started going to church more than ever. He became the African American man that his mother, Rachel Voss, raised him to be. Voss stays out of trouble and carries himself in a respectable way. This book tells his story.